Business Start-up in the Digital Age
Smart Ways to a Successful Launch

The digital age can be a huge blessing for anyone who ꝟ willing to take advantage of the vast amount of technolo. Internet, e-mail and personal computers; together with ı make business start-up so much easier than it was a mere ɔ

ı he ᵥn business. It covers software

This book will show readers how to successfully launch thei. ᵥn business. It covers several different scenarios. It will help those who have invented a new product and want to bring it to market. As an alternative, it will help people who intend to sell an existing product that is available locally or can be imported. It will then offer suggestions on starting a service business. For those who don't have any ideas on what kind of business they want to start, it will help them find something appropriate.

Readers will get hints on researching the market for their product or service. It will then cover the choice of a business name and different forms of legal structure. It provides hints on using their residence to operate their business and if that's not possible, it covers some of the issues regarding commercial and retail leases.

Employees can make or break a business and this book shows start-up entrepreneurs how to calculate their human resource requirements and get the most out of their workers.

This book will cover online and offline advertising together with marketing; how to set up a Web site and sell online.

It shows readers how to calculate how much money it will cost to start their business and whether they can self-finance it or obtain money from friends, family or through crowdfunding.

Finally, it reviews different software packages for creating a business plan and then shows readers how to use it, if they need to obtain outside financing.

This book covers all the essentials new entrepreneurs need to successfully launch their own business in the digital age.

Business Start-up in the Digital Age

Smart Ways to a Successful Launch

Published by:
PRODUCTIVE PUBLICATIONS

By
Learn2succeed.com

Incorporated

ISBN: 978-1-55270-522-3

Written by:
Learn2succeed.com Incorporated

Published in Canada by:
Productive Publications, P.O. Box 7200
Station A, Toronto, ON. M5W 1X8
Phone: (416) 483-0634   Fax: (416) 322-7434
Canadian Web Site: *www.ProductivePublications.ca*
American Web Site: *www.ProductivePublications.com*

Front Cover Art:
Spider web adapted from copyright free clip art from *Corel Gallery 200,000*
Corel Corporation, 1600 Carling Ave. Ottawa

Library and Archives Canada Cataloguing in Publication

Business start-up in the digital age: smart ways to a successful launch / by
Learn2succeed.com, Incorporated.

Issued in print and electronic formats.
ISBN 978-1-55270-522-3 (pbk.).--ISBN 978-1-55270-533-0 (pdf).--
ISBN 978-1-55270-524-7 (epub)

1. New business enterprises. 2. Internet. 3. Success in business.
4. Entrepreneurship. I. Learn2succeed.com Inc., author

HD62.5.B883 2014   658.1'1   C2014-904527-1
                                       C2014-904528-X

Disclaimer

This book mentions the names of a number of publicly traded companies, software publishers as well as private businesses. These are provided only by way of example and are not a solicitation to make investments in them; purchase or sell such securities or to purchase the products they offer. Readers should consult a qualified financial advisor before making any investment or purchase decisions.

No representation is made with respect to the accuracy or completeness of the contents of this book and both the author and the publisher specifically disclaim any implied warranties of merchantability or fitness for any particular purpose and in no event shall either be liable for any loss of profit or any other commercial damage; including but not limited to special, incidental, consequential or other damages.

CONTENTS

INTRODUCTION
Use Technology to Your Advantage

Chapter 1
Eureka! You've Invented a New Product

Chapter 2
Manufacture or Sell an Existing Product

Chapter 3
Start a Service Business

Chapter 4
If You Don't Already Have a Business Idea
Use the Internet to Find One!

Chapter 5
Use the Internet to Research Your Potential Market

Chapter 6
Choose a Great Name, then Register
or Incorporate Your Business

Chapter 7
Where to Locate Your Business

Chapter 8
Use the Internet to Source Your Equipment Needs

Chapter 9
Use Your Computer to Prepare
Your Human Resource Plan

Chapter 10
Use Your Computer to Prepare
Your Advertising and Marketing Plan

Chapter 11
Create Your Own Web Site and Sell Online

Chapter 12
Cash Flow is Your Lifeblood!

Chapter 13
Use Your Computer to Find Out How Much Money
You Will Need to Start

Chapter 14
Use Your Computer to Prepare Your Business Plan

Chapter 15
Track Your Progress
and Be Prepared to Modify Your Business Plan

INTRODUCTION

Use Technology to Your Advantage

We Live in Interesting Times

An ancient Chinese curse said: "may you live in interesting times." One thing is for sure is the times we live in are "interesting" but that is definitely not a curse. In fact, the digital age can be a huge blessing to anyone who wants to start a business and can take advantage of the vast amount of technology currently at our disposal.

I may be ageing myself, but when I started my first business about 35 years ago, there was no Internet, e-mail and personal computers were just in their infancy. I remember how proud I was when I purchased my first Commodore 64 which, at that time, was at the cutting edge of technology. I remember using this new gizmo to write one of my first books and it consisted of a huge number of small files that consisted of about four pages of text each and had to be linked together in order to create the book which I was authoring.

How Things Have Changed!

I am dictating this paragraph using Dragon voice dictation software and, if I get my thoughts together, I can dictate at almost 160 words per minute, which would challenge the abilities of most speed-typists. This software could save you hours and hours of time when you have a lot of writing to do, such as preparing a business plan or writing a report or preparing a press release. This is just one example of a program that can make your life so much easier in our current digital world.

There are many other software programs that can help you at business start-up as well as during the early stages of operations. I'll cover many of these later in this book but they cover everything from business planning, billing and accounting software, contact management, time planning, desktop publishing, preparing brochures; to name but a few.

The Internet came into existence about 25 years ago and it has made a huge difference for businesses of all shapes and sizes. It is an invaluable help at the early start-up stages for doing market research, for finding suppliers, for advertising and promoting your products or services through your own Web sites. You can take it a stage further and create your own e-commerce site where you can take orders from people in your local market as well as from anywhere in the world; assuming that your product would appeal to people in foreign markets.

Being able to advertise your products and sell them over the Internet 24-hours a day; 7-days a week; 52-weeks a year was something that simply was not possible 25 plus years ago.

You Don't Have to Be a Computer Geek!

Most of the software that I mentioned above does not require you to have taken a course at university or college in computer science. Most of these programs are very easy to learn. I can vouch for that, because I certainly do not consider myself a computer geek.

Having said all of this, learning some of these programs can take time and effort on your part but the dividends can be enormous in terms of the efficiency with which you can run your new business. With some of the trickier pieces of software, I have attended evening courses at school to help me get the hang of how some software programs work and how I could use them to my advantage. In addition, I have used instruction manuals, video learning courses (some of which accompany the programs) and others are available from third-party vendors at relatively modest cost.

Computers Have Already Revolutionized Certain Industries

The publishing industry has undergone a huge transformation over the past 35 years and a lot of content is now available in digital format e.g. e-books, e-magazines and e-newspapers. Video and film making have been transformed through the use of digital editing and post-production. The design and drafting profession have moved away from large drafting boards to computer aided design (CAD). The retailing industry has been making rapid shifts from bricks-and-mortar stores to e-commerce over the Internet.

Education is also undergoing a transformation as more colleges and universities are offering degree courses online which enable people from all around the world to attend. Indeed, you can now obtain a degree from a prestigious university without ever having to set foot on the campus.

These are just a few examples of changes that have taken place which have had a dramatic effect on the way in which business is done and it's up to you to take advantage of them when you are starting your own business.

You Ain't Seen Nothing Yet!

Yes, there's more to come!

The 3-D printing Revolution is just getting started. It has very rapidly moved from creating three-dimensional signs to creating prototypes of a great variety of different products and at very low cost compared to years gone by. As you have probably read in the press, 3-D printing is being used to create body parts such as the ears or parts of organs to replace damaged areas. General Electric, the huge American multinational company, is using 3-D printing in many of its manufacturing processes.

The cost of 3-D printers is coming down rapidly every day and there is no reason why start-up entrepreneurs cannot use this technology to help create new products and test them on the marketplace before making any commitments to purchase expensive manufacturing equipment.

Manufacturing robots have been around for quite a number of years and most are quite different from the original R2-D2 of Star Wars science fiction. They are now standard fair in automobile manufacturing production lines as well as for assembly of electronic products and components. Many of these pieces of equipment have involved substantial outlays of cash, however, the cost of small assembly robots has come down dramatically and are now within the financial reach of many small business operators.

The obvious advantage of robots is that they can work 24-hours a day, don't complain about working conditions; they don't belong to a union; they don't show up late for work when the weather is too hot or too cold and they don't require medical insurance (although they do break down every now and again). You don't have to pay them a Christmas bonus and in fact, you don't even have to smile and be nice to them!

Use the Digital World to Your Advantage

In this brief introduction, I have provided a small glimpse of what lies out there in the digital world that can be an enormous benefit to you in starting a new business. These digital technologies, software and equipment do not necessarily cost an arm and a leg. Most are within the financial reach of many start-up entrepreneurs and they can be leveraged to make the business start-up much less tedious than was the case nearly 35 years ago when I first started my own business.

You will find that you have to be a Jack-of-all-trades when you begin to run your own business. You have to be a business planner; a marketing expert; an advertising specialist; a production manager; a bookkeeper; an accountant, a human resource manager and so on. All of these functions can be quite intimidating at the start-up stage but you can take advantage of the digital world to try and make your debut as smooth as possible.

What I will try to do in the course of this short book, is to steer you in the right direction so that you can take advantage of technology in creating your business.

Sadly, many businesses fail during the first couple of years of operation because the start-up business owners do not have the expertise; the knowledge or the experience to survive in a cut-throat world. This is why many franchisees are more successful when they operate under a large franchise operation which can train them how to run their business successfully and make money. In spite of this, I have run across franchisees that have been unsuccessful, so it is not a panacea to start a franchise operation, in addition to which you have to toe the line in accordance with your franchise agreement.

When you run your own business you are not under any external constraints, however, the learning process can be full of traps and pitfalls. In this regard, technology may be able to help you by eliminating some of the mundane tasks and allowing you to focus on the big picture i.e., getting your business up and running and making it profitable.

How this Book Can Help You

I have tried to design this book in such a way that it can cover a number of different scenarios at the business formation stage. I realize that a one-size-fits-all does not work, so the initial chapters are written to address different situations.

Chapter 1 will help you if you have invented a new product and want to bring it to market. The second chapter will cover situations where you intend to sell an existing product that is already available; either locally or can be imported. The third chapter will cover businesses which offer a service. The fourth chapter will help you if you don't have any ideas on what kind of business you want to start and it will help you to come up with something that is appropriate to your circumstances.

Once you have come up with a product or service, you will need to find out if there is a market for it. The fifth chapter will help you do this. Obviously, there's no point in wasting a lot of time, effort and money on something that will not sell and you may have to go back to the drawing board.

The sixth chapter will help you go through the process of registering or incorporating your business and the importance of coming up with a suitable name.

The next chapters will help you determine what your space requirements will be or whether you can operate out of your home. They will also help you if you have to source equipment and determine how many employees you need.

Find out how to use your computer to prepare your advertising and marketing plans. Learn to create your own Web site and, if appropriate, find out how to conduct e-commerce so that you can sell your products online.

The next part of the book gets down to the nitty-gritty of running your business. It will provide you with some help in preparing your sales projections and pricing your product on the market. It will also help you to figure out your fixed and variable costs and how to prepare your cash flow projections. Once you have reached that stage, you will be able to figure out how much money you will need to start your business and whether you can manage by using your own funds or if you will have to seek outside investors or lenders.

You will now have reached the most critical part and that is, assembling all of the information that you have gathered and creating your own business plan. You will also be shown how to use it to assist you in obtaining debt or equity financing.

As you can see, most of the above discussion involves the use of computer software or the Internet. These are incredibly powerful tools and every new business owner should use them if they want to launch their business successfully. So, use the digital world to your advantage when you're starting your own business!

Chapter 1

Eureka! You've Invented a New Product

How Do You Protect Your Invention?

Okay, so you jump out of your bath tub and run down the street naked shouting "Eureka!"

So, how do you stop everybody on the street copying your idea and leave you without a penny to show for all your efforts?

Well, there are various ways in which to protect your idea or invention. You can file for patent protection, copyright or protect your design.

I'll show you how you can do each of these in the following sections.

How Can Patents Protect You?

Patents are a grant by governments giving you the right to exclude others from making, using or selling your invention.

Patents in the USA

For the USA, patents can be filed with the United States Patent and Trademark Office (USPTO) which is an agency of the Department of Commerce and provides a precise description as follows: "A patent is a property right granted by the Government of the United States of America to an inventor 'to exclude others from making, using, offering for sale, or selling the invention throughout the United States or importing the invention into the United States' for a limited time in exchange for public disclosure of the invention when the patent is granted."

The USPTP outlines what can be patented. It states that utility patents are provided for a new, non-obvious and useful:

- process
- machine
- article of manufacture
- composition of matter
- improvement of any of the above

In addition to utility patents, encompassing one of the categories above, patent protection is available for (1) ornamental design of an article of manufacture or (2) asexually reproduced plant varieties by design and plant patents.

USPTO outlines what cannot be patented:

- laws of nature
- physical phenomena

- abstract ideas
- literary, dramatic, musical, and artistic works (these can be Copyright protected)
- inventions which are not useful (such as perpetual motion machines); or offensive to public morality

USPTO states that the invention must also be:

- novel
- non-obvious
- adequately described or enabled (for one of ordinary skill in the art to make and use the invention)
- claimed by the inventor in clear and definite terms

How Do You Know If Your Invention Is Patentable?

First, your should review the list of what can and cannot be patented and determine if your invention falls into one of those categories.

Second, learn the basics of the patenting process from the materials provided by the USPTO by phone at: 1-800-PTO-9199 or 703-308-HELP or under "General Information."

The USPTO goes on: "Next, a search of all previous public disclosures (prior art) including, but not limited to previously patented inventions in the US (prior art) should be conducted to determine if your invention has been publicly disclosed and thus is not patentable. A search of foreign patents and printed publications should also be conducted. While a search of the prior art before the filing of an application is not required, it is advisable to do so. A registered attorney or agent is often a useful resource for performance of a patentability search. After an application is filed, the USPTO will conduct a search as part of the official examination process.

Conducting a thorough patent search is difficult, particularly for the novice. Patent searching is a learned skill. The best advice for the novice is to contact the nearest Patent and Trademark Resource Center (PTRC) and seek out search experts to help in setting up a search strategy. If you are in the Washington, D.C. area, the USPTO provides public access to collections of patents, trademarks, and other documents at its Search Facilities located in Alexandria, Virginia."

How Long Does US Patent Protection Last?

For applications filed on or after June 8, 1995, utility and plant patents are granted for a term which begins with the date of the grant and usually ends 20 years from the date you first applied for the patent subject to the payment of appropriate maintenance fees for a utility patent. There are no maintenance fees for plant patents. Design patents last 14 years from the date you are granted the patent. No maintenance fees are required for design patents.

Patents in force on June 8, 1995 and patents issued thereafter on applications filed prior to June 8, 1995 automatically have a term that is the greater of the twenty-year term discussed above or seventeen years from the patent grant.

How Much Does it Cost to Get a US Patent?

Fees vary depending on the type of patent application you submit. Fees may also vary according to the way you "claim" your invention.

There are three basic fees for utility patents.

The filing fee, which is non-refundable whether or not a patent is granted. (This is the cost to have your invention "examined" by the US Patent and Trademark Office - remember, you may or may not get a patent!)

The issue fee (you pay this only if your application is allowed).

Maintenance fees (paid at 3 1/2, 7 1/2, and 11 1/2 years after your patent is granted - these fees "maintain" your legal protection).

Additional fees may be required.

The USPTO strongly advises you to check the current fee schedule before submitting your application. Having said that, you will probably find that filing a patent costs upwards of $14,000.

What Is a PCT Application?

The Patent Cooperation Treaty (PCT) is an international agreement for filing patent applications having effect in many countries around the world. Although the PCT system does not provide for the grant of "an international patent," the system simplifies the process of filing patent applications, delays the expenses associated with applying for patent protection in foreign countries, and allows the inventor more time to assess the commercial viability of his/her invention. Under the PCT, an inventor can file a single international patent application in one language with one patent office, in order to simultaneously seek protection for an invention in the PCT member countries.

Further Information on Patenting in the USA

Commissioner for Patents
P.O. Box 1450
Alexandria, VA 22313-1450
USA

Patents in Canada

Patents within Canada last for a period of 20 years from the date of filing.

In Canada, patents can be obtained by making application to:

Canadian Intellectual Property Office (CIPO)
Place du Portage I
50 Victoria St., Room C-114
Gatineau, QC   K1A 0C9
Phone toll-free: 1-(866) 997-1936
Fax: (819) 953-2476

Patents in Plain Speak

You should first ascertain that your invention has not already been patented through an examination of the patent files. So, if you have developed a new gizmo, you must try to find out if somebody else has beaten you to the punch and has already developed your idea. This may not matter if they have not taken legal steps to protect their invention, but if they have a patent or have applied for one, you could be in trouble. You have to be careful to check and see that you are not infringing on anyone else's patent.

A classic example of patent infringement was provided by two former giants--Polaroid and Kodak over the instant camera. Polaroid was successful in its claim before the American courts that there had been a violation of its patent with the result that it was able to force Kodak to withdraw from the instant camera market.

You can have patent searches done through a patent attorney, however, a somewhat less expensive procedure is to approach the Canadian Industrial Innovation Centre in Waterloo, Ontario. For a modest fee, an initial evaluation will be made. If this is successful, a further evaluation will be conducted. This procedure is designed to reduce a lot of the time that is frequently wasted on unpatentable ideas, or ones that have already been patented.

After your search has been completed, your patent application and fee is sent to Ottawa. This usually includes technical drawings and descriptions and is normally prepared by a patent agent. It will take two to three years for processing to be completed; during which time amendments to the application may be required.

If all is successful and upon payment of a final fee, your patent will be issued. Total cost for a simple patent will be upwards of $5,000 for Canada and more then $14,000 for both Canada and the United States.

Remember that if you are successful in obtaining a successful patent in Canada or the United States, it will not protect your product outside of those areas.

As you will realize, worldwide patent protection can be a costly and time-consuming procedure. The merits of such an expense will have to be weighed very carefully, however, a product with exclusive world patent rights will certainly make many of your potential investors sit up and take notice.

Copyright

Copyright--or the right to copy--means that the owner of the work is the only one who may copy it or permit someone else to do so.

"Work" means any original literary, dramatic, musical, or artistic effort and includes such things as books, magazines, films, etc. "Copying" means printing, photocopying, reproducing, performing and the use of mechanical contrivances such as records, cassettes and tapes. Things such as computer software can also be copyrighted.

Copyright in the USA

According to the US Copyright Office: "Copyright is a form of protection provided by the laws of the United States to the authors of 'original works of authorship,' including literary, dramatic, musical, artistic, and certain other intellectual works. This protection is available to both published and unpublished works....The Copyright Act generally gives the owner of copyright the exclusive right to do and to authorize others to do the following:

- reproduce the work in copies or phonorecords;
- prepare derivative works based upon the work;
- distribute copies or phonorecords of the work to the public by sale or other transfer of ownership, or by rental, lease, or lending;
- perform the work publicly, in the case of literary, musical, dramatic, and horeographic works, pantomimes, and motion pictures and other audio-visual works;
- display the work publicly, in the case of literary, musical, dramatic, and horeographic works, pantomimes, and pictorial, graphic, or sculptural works, including the individual images of a motion picture or other audio visual work; perform the work publicly (in the case of sound recordings) by means of a digital audio transmission.

In addition, certain authors of works of visual art have the rights of attribution and integrity as described in section 106A of the 1976 Copyright Act."

"It is illegal for anyone to violate any of the rights provided by the copyright law to the owner of copyright... limitations are specified exemptions from copyright liability. One major limitation is the doctrine of 'fair use.'"

"Fair Use" and "Fair Dealing"

Fair use is a contentious issue which has been fought over in the courts. In Canada, it landed up in the Supreme Court.

In Canada, according to The Canadian Copyright Licensing Agency (ACESS) "students enrolled in a class and that each student can print a copy (whether 20 or 500 students). At the same time, the policy does not allow a professor to photocopy multiple copies of an article for distribution to students. In other words, the AUCC Fair Dealing Policy appears to allow faculty, staff and students to do indirectly what they cannot do directly."

I'll revert to Wickipedia which states that "In United States copyright law, fair use is a doctrine that permits limited use of copyrighted material without acquiring permission from the rights holders. Examples of fair use include commentary, search engines, criticism, parody, news reporting, research, teaching, library archiving and scholarship. It provides for the legal, unlicensed citation or incorporation of copyrighted material in another author's work under a four-factor balancing test."

Further Information on Copyright in the USA

Library of Congress
Copyright Office-COPUBS
101 Independence Avenue S.E.
Washington, DC 20559
Phone: (202) 707-3000
Phone toll-free: 1-(877) 476-0778

Copyright in Canada

Generally, copyright lasts for a period of 50 years. It is automatically conferred at the time an original work is created in Canada, however, if you are serious about it, you should register with the Federal Government. The fee is modest and the forms are relatively simple to complete.

For information or forms, you should contact:

Copyright Board of Canada
Suite 800 - 56 Sparks Street
Ottawa, ON K1A 0C9
Phone: (613) 952 8621 Fax: (613) 952-8630
E-mail: secretariat@cb-cda.gc.ca
Web site: http://www.cb-cda.gc.ca

Once your application has been processed you will be issued with a "Certificate of Registration" which can be used in a court of law to support any claim.

Unlike patents, copyright confers on your rights, as holder, in other countries that are members of the Berne Copyright Convention or the Universal Copyright Convention. So, copyright is a relatively inexpensive way of protecting your work in a major portion of the Western World.

The Significance of Patent or Copyright Protection

There is considerable debate as to how valuable patents and copyrights are to a company. Frequently, they can be circumvented or simply become irrelevant because the technology is moving so fast that they become obsolete.

One thing you have to be very careful about is to make sure that you are not infringing on someone else's patent because you could be laying yourself open to legal action by the patent holder. The technology business is awash with patent infringement suits often involving very large companies and the penalties or settlements can run into the millions of dollars.

If you are self-financing your own business, whether you have a patent or not, may be of little concern, although it does expose you to the risk that someone will steal your idea. However, if you reach the point of looking for an outside investor the question takes on much more significance.

The investor is likely to obtain considerable comfort from knowing that you have some protection for the product that is being financed. So, if you have obtained such protection or are in the application process, it would be wise for you to emphasize this in any documents or letters which you use to seek financing.

The same thing is true of copyrights.

Register Trademarks

A trade-mark is a word, a symbol, a design (or a combination) used to distinguish your wares or services from those of others in the market. It represents not only your goods and services, but also the reputation of your business. If you propose to use a Trademark, I would advise you to register it. In Canada, this can be done online at the Canadian Intellectual Property Office (CIPO) and in the USA at the United States Patent and Trademark Office.

The Web sites are as follows:

Canada: *www.cipo.ic.gc.ca*
USA: *www.uspto.gov*

Create a Working Prototype

If you have invented a new gizmo, one of the first things that you have to do, if at all possible, is to create a working prototype.

If this is something that costs a lot of money you may be able to get government assistance under the IRAP Program of the National Research Council of Canada and further information under the America Invents Act at the US Patent Office by phone: (571)-272-1000.

You may be able to attract informal investors to put some money in the pot. Obviously, it would be at your best interest to try to attain a patent protection before you do this, since there are unscrupulous investors out there who may attempt to run off with your idea.

Chapter 2

Manufacture or Sell an Existing Product

Set Yourself Up as a Manufacturer of an Existing Product

If you're going to manufacture an existing product, you will have to make sure that you're not violating any existing patents or designs of other manufacturers of the same product, otherwise you could be laying yourself open to legal action.

If you're going to take this road, you'll need to try and find out as much as you can about the manufacturing process and if there are more efficient ways to produce the product at a lower cost. If you are unable to do this you will be at a disadvantage in the marketplace.

Don't forget that existing manufacturers have probably written off the cost of their equipment. In your case, you may be at a disadvantage if the capital cost of the equipment is high and you have to recover that cost during the initial years of your operation.

You also have to determine whether there is enough room in the market for you to compete with other companies which are making the same product. Don't forget that they will probably not welcome you and may lower their prices in an attempt to try and squeeze you out of their market.

On the other hand, if the market is under-served, there may be a good opportunity for you to start a profitable business.

The key is to do as much research as you possibly can before you dive head-first into the marketplace.

Sell a Domestically Produced Product

You can also set up a business to sell a domestically produced product and act as a sales agent, dealer, distributor or a wholesaler. This could be a very easy way to start a business if a product is already well accepted in certain areas of the country such as a province or state. You will have the advantage of seeing how others are performing in their areas; thereby greatly reducing your risk of entry.

Sell Imported Products

If you can find products abroad that are not available in your local market, you may be able to start a profitable business for yourself. I did this for myself a number of years ago and I found an amazing number of products that were not available in my local market.

Be aware that tastes vary from country to country. In addition, there are also regulations about packaging and labelling.

Air Cargo

I've used air cargo or air freight quite a lot in the past before the rapid run-up in oil prices. You may find the rates are currently cost-prohibitive except for high value, lightweight electronic items.

With oil prices having come down a little, and carriers scrambling for business, air cargo may once again become a viable alternative for importing goods especially if they are needed fast. I used to bring fairly light-weight plastic components from Philadelphia to Toronto by air cargo and ended up paying only a slight premium over the rates by truck, which of course took a lot longer.

I also remember, a number of years ago, a customer in Brazil wanted 200 books shipped by FedEx. I told them I thought that I could do better than that if they were prepared to pick up the goods at San Paulo airport. Indeed, non-priority air freight (without the 2-day delivery guarantee) cost only about one-third of the Fed-Ex rate.

Another factor you should consider with air cargo, especially for goods imported from Asia or Europe, is the time you have your money tied up and interest costs while you wait for them to arrive by surface (which could take several months).

Truck

Most United States-Canada-Mexico freight is handled by truck. The service is well-established. I've used trucks regularly in the past and freight companies will consolidate your order with those of other customers.

The key is to find a freight forwarder that specializes in the route so that you do not have delays with multiple carriers which can cause problems with damaged or lost goods, and so on. Again, I remember there was one carrier I used regularly on the Philadelphia to Toronto run.

Currently, Mainfreight USA offers a dedicated overnight service from major Eastern US cities to Canada. This can be for either full truckload or less than truckload.

Containers

If you are importing goods by surface from Europe or Asia, probably the best way is by container. The obvious advantage is that these can be transported by truck or rail to the port of departure; by sea on a container ship and then by road or rail from the receiving port.

Containers are of two basic sizes: 20 foot or 40 foot; with 20 foot being the most common. Now, a 20 foot container can carry a lot of merchandise so you may want to use the services of a consolidated freight company which will pack your cartons along with those of others going to the same destination.

There are many companies in this business and again, my advice is to choose one which specializes in services from the foreign destination to your local area.

Post, UPS, FedEx, DHL

Don't laugh! Plain old parcel post will work well for small quantities of imported goods. By air mail, the service tends to be very expensive and not that fast–two weeks or more is not uncommon. The service by surface is as slow as molasses but on the other hand it can be relatively inexpensive. One caveat–make sure that you pay the extra for insurance coverage since tracking is only offered on some routes and, from bitter experience, I can tell you that cartons have a habit of "disappearing" so make sure that at least you get your money back, even if it takes an eternity to extract it from your postal service.

UPS, FedEx and DHL are all legitimate parcel and courier companies you can use for importing your merchandise. They have good parcel tracking capabilities but I find that, with the exception of UPS, they tend to be rather expensive.

One thing I have found with UPS, is that if you have a lot of cartons coming from one destination to the same address, a discount kicks in which often makes the service less expensive than using the post. Check it out!

NAFTA

As you know, there is a free trade agreement between Canada, Mexico and the USA. Yea...Right! There may be zero duty rates on the stuff you are importing but you'll still have tons of paperwork. Of course, if you are in Canada, the Feds want to collect the HST, even if it's just a minimal amount. The concept of an open border for goods flowing between countries, such as is the case in Europe, does not apply in North America which employs vast numbers of bureaucrats to obstruct the free flow. So much for "free" trade, North American style!

Politicos–are you listening? Probably not!

Do-it-Yourself Customs Clearance

If your goods are arriving by post, I would certainly clear them yourself. Canada Post levies a $5.00 charge and will collect the duties and HST payable based on the customs declaration. If you don't agree, you can refuse to accept the goods and have them cleared in front of a customs officer. Quite frankly for the time and bother involved, I have frequently paid the duties even though I wanted to dispute them. It depends on how much value you place on your time.

The US Postal Service is also supposed to levy a fee for collecting duties on imported goods but from what I gather can be quite lax about it.

Customs Brokers

The role of the customs broker is to clear the goods through customs on your behalf. When I operated an import business a number of years ago, I relied on them heavily and I found the service well worthwhile. Essentially, your broker will do all the paperwork and pay the duties and any taxes on your behalf. Be warned, however, that they want their money fast for performing this service–so it's pay immediately on receipt of their invoice!

I operated out of Toronto and many of the goods coming in by truck would enter via Fort Erie or Niagara Falls. It simply was not practical for me to travel there, fill out all the paperwork, wait in a line to clear the goods. It was much easier to pay a relatively small amount to a customs broker to perform that service for me.

The broker which I used, also had an office at the air freight terminal at Toronto Pearson Airport, so they could also handle customs clearance on incoming air freight shipments. Yes–use the services of a customs broker!

Paying for Imported Goods

There are a number of ways to pay for imported goods and I'll give you a brief run down in the following sections.

Cash in Advance (CIA)

Payment by cash in advance obviously benefits an exporter. He is receiving the funds prior to shipping the goods and is in effect being financed by the foreign purchaser.

The converse holds true for payments made in advance by an importer. The risk is that the supplier will take off with the money and not supply the goods! Alternatively, the goods may not be up to specification or of poor quality.

Goods may also be shipped late, since the supplier is not under any financial pressure to make shipment in order to receive payment.

The moral of this story is to make sure that your supplier is reputable.

Cash on Delivery (COD)

Cash on Delivery or COD is not a practice one might associate with imports or exports, however, because of the large amount of trade conducted between Canada and the United States, it is an acceptable method of payment for smaller transactions between companies on either side of the border.

COD arrangements are dependent on the carrier. Some freight companies will transport goods on a COD basis, whilst others will avoid it.

An exporter conducting trade on a COD basis should take into account the delivery time for the goods. This is likely to be longer than would be the case for internal shipments made within Canada or the USA (because of delays at the border with customs) and consequently, payment will take longer to be received.

An importer purchasing on a COD basis has the advantage of not having to pay until the goods arrive i.e., they have "credit" while the goods are in transit.

There are several disadvantages of conducting business on this basis. Many carriers will not handle COD shipments and if they do, there are COD charges which have to be absorbed (usually by the purchaser). Problems also arise if goods on COD are not accepted. The return freight costs, handling charges and customs broker costs can add up to a nightmare.

Open Account

Much of the trade between Canada and the United States is done on open account with standard trade terms. When payment becomes due, it is normally made by money order, cheque or draft in the currency of the supplier's country.

This is a risk that the purchaser will not pay for the goods which, in turn, exposes the exporter to possible financial losses. Such practice of selling on open account is obviously dependent on the satisfactory credit rating of the purchaser.

There is, however, a disadvantage on open account that readers should be aware of. This occurs if the terms are shorter than the delivery time for the goods.

Thus, trade terms of "Net 15" days are next to worthless if the goods take 30 days to arrive! If the customer pays on time, he would actually have paid 15 days in advance and would be better off doing business on a COD basis!

The above example may be somewhat extreme, but it serves to illustrate a point. Goods exported over the border tend to take longer to arrive than domestic, because of delays caused by customs. Thus, terms of Net 30 days on goods that took 29 days to arrive would only give an effective trade credit of one day! Not too generous!

These circumstances might lead to American customers seeking extended terms to offset the time spent in transit.

How a Letter of Credit Works

A letter of credit is a negotiable document issued by a bank to facilitate the purchase of imported or exported goods. These documents are one of the most common methods of payment in international trade.

To illustrate the method of operation, I will examine the case of an importer and then an exporter.

Let us say that you wish to import some goods from XYZ Company. You establish a price with the company and then go to your bank and request that they issue a letter of credit in favour of XYZ Company for the amount in question. This letter states that the bank will honour payment to XYZ Company once the goods are delivered. XYZ Company can then take this letter of credit to its own bank and borrow against it.

Depending on your relationship with your bank, it may not debit your account until the actual payment is made, however, it will probably insist that sufficient funds be maintained in your account, at least to cover the amount in question.

Conversely, let us say that you are exporting to ABC Company. You establish a price for the goods. They go to their bank and have a letter of credit issued in your favour. They send you the letter of credit. You ship the goods and you can take the letter of credit to your bank and you may be able to borrow against it until payment is received.

The bank lends its name to the transaction and guarantees that the supplier will be paid, provided that certain conditions are met. These vary according to the type of letter of credit that is issued and are usually a matter for negotiation between the importer and exporter.

Irrevocable Letter of Credit

As its name suggests, an irrevocable letter of credit cannot be changed without the consent of both the purchaser and the seller of the goods.

This is the normal type issued for most transactions between companies that are not related to one another.

Sight Draft

Under this arrangement, the goods are shipped and the shipping documents; together with the sight draft are submitted to the purchaser's bank. The bank then checks the shipping documents, to make sure that they are in order and that the goods were in fact shipped.

Payment is then made on the basis of the draft to the supplier and the documents are released to the purchaser; thereby enabling him to clear the goods through customs and obtain their release from the freight company.

There is a risk to the seller or exporter under this arrangement that the documentation may not be complete or correct, which in turn, would prevent the bank from making payment.

There is also a risk to the seller or exporter that the issuing bank may be unable to honour the letter of credit. This could be the result of political upheaval, war etc.

Term Draft

This arrangement is similar to that for a sight draft, except that instead of payment being made immediately by the purchaser's bank on finding that the documentation is in order; it is made by means of a term draft in which the bank guarantees that it will be made some 30, 60 or 90 days later.

The shipping documents, however, are released so that when the goods arrive at their destination, the purchaser can take possession of them immediately after they have cleared customs.

The terms in such drafts are normally for the period that the goods are in transit. This is equivalent to the supplier allowing the purchaser a period of trade credit equivalent to the period in transportation.

Sellers, under this arrangement are also exposed to the same risk as outlined above under Sight Drafts.

Confirmed Credits

In certain cases (usually in Third World countries), the reliability of the bank or the country in which the bank is located may be questionable. I mentioned this risk in the two arrangements I discussed above.

In this event, another bank can be asked to guarantee the letter of credit by confirming it.

In other words, should the issuing bank fail; the confirming bank would guarantee payment. Letters of credit issued in this manner are referred to as "confirmed credits."

Confirmed Credits may be payable on sight i.e., on presentation of documents or subject to terms in the same manner as I explained above under Sight Drafts or Term Drafts.

Revocable Credits

Revocable credits are only issued for special transactions. Such might be the case where goods are shipped by a parent company to its subsidiary.

In this type of arrangement, the terms of the letter of credit can be changed by the supplier without having to consult the purchaser in advance.

Financing with Bankers Acceptances

When a term draft is issued (see above), it is a negotiable instrument that promises payment in 30, 60, 90 or even 180 days. Such a draft is known as a banker's acceptance, because as a negotiable instrument, it can be presented to a bank before the time that it becomes due. The normal size of a banker's acceptance is $100,000 and up.

Such an arrangement allows the supplier to take the draft to his bank and obtain full payment, less a discount calculated on the interest to maturity. It enables the supplier to obtain his funds at a discount.

A Word of Warning on Letters of Credit

I should issue a word of warning about the use of letters of credit from the importer's viewpoint.

They only insure that goods are shipped and delivered. They do not contain any warranty as to the quality of the goods. The purchaser is not covered against poor quality or bad workmanship.

Payment will always be made so long as the documents are in order (unless fraud can be proven and poor workmanship may be difficult to prove as fraud).

The only way you can overcome this, is by dealing exclusively with respectable suppliers or by insisting on an independent inspection in the country of origin. This will ensure that goods are up to standard.

Be warned, however, that inspectors carrying out such inspections are also subject to bribery! *Caveat emptor*!

From the exporter's viewpoint, letters of credit are only good if the documents (bill of lading) are made available to the confirming bank.

In countries where there is political disturbance or civil unrest, those documents may not become available--hence no payment! In other words, they do not provide an ironclad guarantee that payment will be made.

Collections

A collection is simply an arrangement under which an exporter will have its bank collect the money due on a transaction. The two most common types of collections are as follows.

Documents on Payment

When the exporter ships the goods, he hands the documents to his bank, which in turn, forwards them to a correspondent bank in the foreign country. That foreign bank will then supply the documents to the purchaser against payment. Armed with the documents, the purchaser can obtain customs clearance of the goods and their release from the transportation company.

This is almost equivalent to a COD transaction, except that banks act as the collecting agent, instead of the freight company.

There is, however, a danger in this arrangement that the exporter should be aware of. What happens if the importer suddenly decides that he does not want the goods and the exporter is faced with the cost of bringing them back home at his expense? This can be very costly in the case of overseas transactions.

As with Letters of Credit, the purchaser is also exposed to the possible shipment of shoddy or poor quality goods.

Documents on Acceptance

This is similar to the documents against payment method, except that a period of trade credit (such as 30, 60 or 90 days) is allowed. To obtain the shipping documents from the bank, the purchaser must sign a draft for the amount and the term in question. When the draft matures, the purchaser pays the bank; which in turn remits payment to the exporter.

Financing is possible under this arrangement. Credit may be extended by the bank to the exporter until payment is received. Alternatively, the bank may be prepared to accept such drafts as collateral for a short-term loan.

The converse holds true for the importer; insofar as he is obtaining trade credit for the 30, 60 or 90 days in question.

Again, the purchaser is exposed to the risk of being shipped poor quality goods.

The buyer may refuse (or be unable) to pay for the goods at the expiry of the term. This could lead to legal proceedings, since title of the goods has already passed to the purchaser. These legal proceedings could be expensive and time-consuming if they have to be conducted in a foreign country with all the possible language and legal differences.

Forfaiting

Forfaiting is a financing technique used by exporters, usually involving large transactions with respect to capital equipment. Under such an arrangement, a bank (or finance house) will purchase medium-term foreign payment obligations. Such purchases are made at a discount from their face value.

Such an arrangement has the advantage of providing the exporter with cash in respect of payments that he is waiting for over the next 2-5 years. It also has the advantage of protecting the importer against future currency devaluations, since that becomes the problem of the bank or the company that purchased the obligations.

Countertrade

Countertrade involves the straight exchange of goods; with or without the presence of a middleman or agent. Essentially, it is a fancy name for bartering - "You got two goats--I got one cow. We do deal?"

Such trade is worth about $1.2 billion annually in Canada. It is mostly conducted by companies selling high technology, military hardware or those that make a living out of international trading.

Usually, countertrade deals involve amounts in excess of $1 million, which puts them out of range of most small businesses.

Export Leasing

Export leasing is a technique which can be used to obtain a competitive advantage in the market of the country to which the goods are being sold. Such arrangements are normally made with leasing companies in the foreign country in conjunction with a chartered bank.

Buyer Credits

Buyer credits are sometimes involved when purchases are made of large pieces of equipment or other capital goods. Thus, if an exporter loans money to its foreign customer to facilitate the purchase of the goods; such an arrangement is known as a "buyer credit".

Frequently, such loans are guaranteed by the government or a bank in the country of the purchaser.

Supplier Credits

This is a method of financing exports. Under this arrangement, a bank buys (usually at a discount) the promissory notes issued by the purchaser of the goods. Frequently such notes are the subject of government guarantees against non-payment.

Chapter 3

Start a Service Business

Services Can Cover a Wide Spectrum

Services can cover a wide spectrum; all the way from retail stores, restaurants, real estate agencies, financial services; to name but a few. They also cover care of the elderly, landscaping auto repair, painters, window cleaners and a vast variety of maintenance people.

Indeed, the service areas cover so many areas and employ so many people that they are a very important employer.

Since this book is about starting a business in the digital age, I will try to confine my comments to some areas where computers play a significant role.

Selling Real Estate

If you are selling real estate you will have to be licensed in the areas you work in.

Computers can certainly play a role in letting potential purchasers find out about properties that are up for sale by displaying pictures of the exterior and interior of the property on a computer at the real estate agent's office or online on the Internet.

Computers also make it possible to sift through large numbers of properties in order to select the ones that are of most interest to the purchaser in terms of what they are looking for e.g., number of bedrooms, bathrooms, proximity of schools, etc.

Bricks-and-Mortar Retail Stores

Computers come into their own into signing store layouts, preparing stores signage and in planogramming. I'll try and explain briefly.

You don't have to be a rocket scientist to analyse your store's performance. You can take the figures from your cash register departments and use them to calculate your sales per square foot by department (referred to as planogramming). Sometimes this analysis can be quite revealing, particularly if it is combined with gross margins to come up with a profit picture on a square foot basis by department in your store.

Now, you don't have to have "departments" as in a department store. You can perform this analysis by product section or by the positioning of products within your store.

I'll provide a simple example. Suppose you have a section devoted to mens' shaving needs--all the way from blades to shaving creams to after-shave lotion. Work out what sales and gross profits you make and then divide by the number of square feet the display occupies. *Voila!* You have your sales and profits per square foot for mens' shaving needs.

Suppose you also offer greeting cards. Perform the same exercise and you'll come up with your sales and profits per square foot of greeting card space.

Take a large sheet of squared paper. Draw out your store layout to an approximate scale together with the fixturing. Use colouring to fill in your sales per square foot. Use blue for areas where you are making a profit per square foot and red where you are making a loss. It can be quite revealing!

Try changing the position of slow moving items to see if that makes any difference--if not–put them on clearance sale and bring in some different merchandise to replace them.

You will also want to try to find out how many times you turned your merchandise over during the year. Did you sell out the display rack one time, three times or ten times? This can usually only be done on a departmental basis in conjunction with figures from the cash register.

If you plan to start a bricks-and-mortar retail business, make sure you use computers to their best advantage!

Restaurants

The restaurant business is a difficult area in which to compete, however, computers can be used all the way from store design, for creating interesting menus, for purchasing food items, etc. They are also invaluable for keeping track of your human resource needs and making sure that you have enough people on hand to service your customers.

Financial Services

Financial services cover a very large area. Unless you have tons of money and are going to start a bank, financial services could involve tax preparation, acting as an insurance agent, providing investment advice (so long as you have the necessary qualifications and are registered).

All these activities involve the use of computers and are very much in the digital world.

Computer Repairs, Installation, Web Design

All of these services are very computer-intensive.

Digital Photography and Film Making

Photography has almost entirely gone digital. The same can be said for film making and post-production. All make heavy use of digital devices and computers.

Book and Magazine Publishing

The entire publishing industry has gone digital; all the way from preparing manuscripts, proofreading to pre-press i.e., preparing material for printing. In addition, huge numbers of books, newspapers and magazines are now available in an electronic format.

There's More and More

What I have covered in this chapter is just a small sample of businesses which are very digital in nature and involve extensive use of computers and the Internet. I am sure that you can think of many others which I have not covered.

Chapter 4

If You Don't Already Have a Business Idea
Use the Internet to Find One!

The Internet

The Internet is a gigantic source of information. It contains billions and billions of "pages" of information; many of which can be useful in market research. Indeed, through the use of what are known as "search engines" it is possible to gather a great deal of specific information very quickly.

Search Engines

There are a large number of search engines which will permit you to "look up" information on the Web. Having said this, five of them dominate the market. Thus, (according to my search on the Web) *eBizMBA* the leading search engines based on usage in April 2014 were as follows:

Google: with 1.1 billion unique monthly visitors.
Bing: with 300 million unique monthly visitors.
Yahoo: with 250 million unique monthly visitors.
Ask: with 145 million unique monthly visitors.
AOL Search: with 75 million unique monthly visitors.

Google commanded the lion's share of the search market with Microsoft's *Bing* a distant second and *Yahoo!* a distant third.

Narrow Down the Search

Google has deservedly earned the reputation of being the most favoured search tool; especially its advanced search feature which permits you to narrow down your search to only those sites containing specific key words or exact phrases. Indeed, at one time or another I have used most of the above sites, but finding sites that are relevant to the query is a challenge. Indeed, general searches can spew out hundreds of thousands of search results; that would take months to go through. *Google's* advanced search feature can help you narrow down the response to a manageable number of relevant sources. Most search engines will let you search for a phrase by placing it in quotation marks.

Your secret to conducting meaningful searches is to select key words that are specific to your search criteria. If you are looking for something that originates from a certain country, province, state or city, it can be helpful to provide that name; otherwise you will get results from all over the world.

On the flip side, you can be so specific in your search that you will not get any results back; especially if searching for a complete phrase. In this instance, you may want to change to a search that contains all the words you have specified (but not necessarily in their exact order in the phrase that you have entered).

One very helpful feature on *Google* is its ability to make a suggestion in the case of an incorrect spelling.

One disadvantage of search sites is the lead positioning of material by people who have paid to have it appear at the beginning of the search results page. The fact that positioning has been paid for, does not always mean that the information is the most relevant.

A word of caution is in place; especially when you are performing advanced searches; and that relates to how up-to-date the information is. Unfortunately, the Web, aside from being an enormous source of the very latest information, is also a repository of huge amounts of redundant information that is completely out of date. Also, many Web sites are poorly maintained with the result that information you uncover can be both inaccurate and out-of-date.

An Example of a Search

A little while back, I performed a search on Google for the words "mouse" and "mouse trap" and came back with up to 13.1 million hits!

> A search for "Mouse Trap" produced 13.1 million hits.
> A search for "Mouse Trap" produced 252,000 hits.
> A search for "Mouse Trap Humane" produced 4,090 hits.
> A search for "Mouse Trap Humane Electric" produced 692 hits.
> A search for "Mouse Trap Humane Electric Canada" produced 181 hits.
> A search for "Mouse Trap Humane Electric Toronto Canada" produced 46 hits.
> A search for the exact phrase: "Humane Electric Mouse Trap" produced no hits.
> A search for the exact phrase "Electric Mouse Trap" produced 21 hits.

It is obvious that there are two extremes in the above example. The word "Mouse Trap" produced so many hits as to be virtually useless. On the other hand, "Humane Electric Mouse Trap" produced no results as an exact phrase and was also of no use. If the word "Humane" was removed, a meaningful number of 21 results were produced.

When I examined the results, some of them related to the mouse as a rodent; one to a cartoon; one to a patent on such a devise; some were funny; some were serious. Obviously, it did not take me long to sift through a small number of results and very often the links on a Web site took me to many other sites that were relevant to my search. Indeed, I was "surfing the net" by going from link to link and in the process uncovering all sorts of useful and relevant information, however, it was also very easy to get off track.

What do People Want?

One of the keys to any business success is to find a need and fill it. This reminds me of an advertisement I saw a number of years ago featuring one of those large cement trucks which deliver concrete to building construction sites. In big letters across the side of the truck it said: "FIND A NEED AND FILL IT".

This is a very simple statement. Think about it!

The need could be anything from wanting to look better by purchasing a snazzy new suit to buying necessities such as food or toothpaste.

Of course, you can think of many items which people purchase which they really don't need. For example, when Imelda Marcos purchased her 1,060[th] pair of shoes, did it really fill a need? Probably...in her mind...and if you were the manufacturer of that pair of shoes...you might have been quite happy to make a few bucks!

I'll leave it to you to figure out what makes a need. It is advertising that "preys" on peoples' needs, their wants, their fears, their prestige, their greed, their sexual desires, etc. It is that perceived need that drives product sales.

So, the first step is to find a need.

Ideas Abound!

I will now show you a number of ways in which to get ideas that you can use to find products to sell through your business. If you have already made up your mind on what you want to do, you may wish to skip this section.

Ideas abound around us and the key to finding something that would be a good fit for you is to go through an initial process of self-examination. You would probably like to work at something which you enjoy even though it may involve a great deal of effort. For example, if you love the outdoors and nature, you might want to take a look at camping equipment. Equally well, if you enjoy golf, you might want to take a look at products which relate to that game.

Let me offer you some suggestions on ways to get ideas. The following sections do not cover every possibility, but they will certainly give you a good handle on how to get started. My advice is to select those which offer the best chances of finding something that fits in with your interests and your skills.

You may find more than one area which would be of interest and I would suggest that you list these. There is certainly no harm in looking at a variety of different areas and in the following steps I will try to help you in doing market research into these areas and to establish which ones would be the most profitable for you to enter into.

Trade Shows

In my own experience, I found trade shows to be a tremendous source of inspiration for new ideas or for ways to make my own products. This is especially true in the gifts and crafts area.

Essentially, trade shows are of two types. There are those that are open to the public, such as many of the sportsman's shows, food shows, home shows and gardening shows, etc., and these are held (usually on an annual basis) in major centres around the country. They are easy to gain access to...all you have to do is pay the entrance fee and you are admitted.

The other type of trade shows are those which specialize in specific industries or services and are intended only for people who work in those areas. In other words, admission is not open to the general public and for that reason I would strongly suggest that you prepare yourself by registering a name for your business and have business cards printed with all your contact information.

Often, a business card is all that is needed to gain admission onsite, however, there is usually an admission fee.

An alternative is to contact the show organizers in advance and request a show registration form which you can complete and e-mail or fax back to the organizer who will then mail you your admission badge. In order to contact the show organizers, I would recommend that you search online and should be able to easily locate trade shows that are held both in North America and throughout the world. A few shows are even presented as virtual or "e-shows" which you can attend online. I have attended several of these but it appears to me that the idea is fading and has not gained much traction.

In the past, I visited many trade shows in Europe, and I have found these to be a great source of inspiration for new ideas or for the creation of new products. Also, many of the products that were on display were not available in North America and this offered many opportunities to introduce these products to the Canadian and US markets. So, I would strongly recommend some foreign travel, if you can afford it, because the further you get away from home, the more likely you are to find products that have not already been developed in your home market.

Many of these trade shows are gigantic in size and I would highly recommend that you plan your visit carefully. Some show organizers will e-mail the exhibitor list in advance or alternatively you can obtain it when you register at the show opening. My suggestion is to go through the list of exhibitors and carefully select those whose products or services that are of interest. You can then target them. To make this easier, most trade shows include a booth layout plan in their exhibitor catalogue which permits you to plan your visits in an organized fashion.

Another alternative is to spend the first day (or two) quickly visiting all the booths without getting involved in any detailed discussions with the salespeople, and make notes on which booths contain products or services that would be of interest to you. In the evenings, you can go through any literature or sales material that you have obtained from those booths and further narrow down your choices. Having done this, you can visit just those companies that meet your criteria and get into detailed discussions with them. Don't forget to exchange business cards and make sure you get Web site addresses.

Be aware that the people manning these booths are trained salespeople who want to close the sale, so be on guard and do not commit yourself to anything until you have had a chance to do your own research and investigate the area more thoroughly.

When you get back home after the show is over, I would recommend that you go through all the literature that you collected and visit the Web sites of the exhibitors. Carefully select anything that would be of interest, even if it involves competitors' products, because such information could be very valuable to you later on. Organize the material and prepare your "to-do" list for follow-ups.

Print-on-Paper Trade Magazines and e-Magazines

Once you have selected the area or areas that you are interested in, I would strongly recommend that you subscribe to the trade magazines and e-magazines which relate to that area. The publishers of many of these magazines may also have booths at the trade shows that relate to them and if you subscribe at the show you may be able to obtain such magazines at a discounted price or for free, provided you meet their circulation criteria (i.e., that you are actively involved in that industry or service since your subscription is being subsidized by the paid advertising contained in the magazine).

I would also suggest that you visit your local reference library which will probably have a number of trade print-on-paper magazines on display. Alternatively, they should be able to provide you with directories that will list trade magazines. Many of these directories are designed to provide information about advertising rates, however, they will also provide you with contact addresses, e-mail addresses, phone and fax numbers so that you can subscribe.

Don't forget to look at foreign publications relating to the area that you're interested in. Thus, there are many trade publications in English that come from Hong Kong, Taiwan, the United Kingdom and other English speaking nations that will give you a different perspective on the area that is of interest to you.

Visit Manufacturers' Web Sites to Get Ideas

Many manufacturers will display their full product lines and pricing on their Web sites. If you want examples, visit the Web sites of the publisher of this book: *www.ProductivePublications.com* if you are in the USA or overseas or *www.ProductivePublications.ca* if you are located in Canada.

Unfortunately, others will hide behind beautiful pictures of "himbos" and "bimbos" and impart little useful information. The ones that are the most infuriating are those which hide behind the clouds in cyberspace and don't provide proper contact information such as address, phone, fax and e-mail addresses. Such businesses are basically saying, "here we are" and "we are great" but don't waste our time by contacting us!

Visit Retail Stores and the Web Sites of Retail Stores to Get Ideas

The shops in your neighbourhood can be a great source of inspiration to create new products. Visit your local shopping mall and you will find millions of ideas for products to sell. You will also see many successful specialty chains that are leaders in their field. These will also give you some idea of what is involved in merchandising and selling products.

I would suggest that you take a small notebook with you and make notes on products or stores that are of interest to you. Be careful not to do this blatantly in front of sales clerks, but rather do it discreetly after you have exited the store. Also, do not attempt to photograph anything, especially in shopping malls, since you will attract the attention of mall security very quickly. Simply put, retailers welcome you as a shopper but can become very hostile if they feel that you are spying on them.

Again, if you have the money to travel, it would be a good idea to examine the merchandise in stores in foreign countries, since these can be a great inspiration for new products that are not available in your local market. A much less expensive way to do this is to go online and visit the Web sites of these stores. If the material is not available in English, the Google search engine can perform a translation for you which may not be perfect, but probably good enough to get a handle on the features and prices of different products.

Catalogues

There are literally thousands upon thousands of catalogues available. Because of the high costs of postage, many are now only available online. For example the publisher of this books offers a free online catalogue which can be downloaded as a PDF file from *www.ProductivePublications.com* if you are in the USA or overseas or *www.ProductivePublications.ca* if you are located in Canada. Once downloaded, they can be viewed or, if you want, printed on your computer printer.

I would classify catalogues into two broad categories: those put out by companies that are selling merchandise which you can purchase directly from the catalogue and those that are put out by manufacturers, distributors, or wholesalers which contain information for those further up the distribution chain. Thus, a manufacturer of widgets might produce a print catalogue or an e-catalogue which describes their full range of widgets so that businesses which sell widgets can be made aware of what is available and how to order them.

Again, depending on your interests, you can obtain copies of these catalogues. Most companies selling merchandise will gladly snail-mail you a copy upon your request in the hope that you will become a customer.

Drop-Ship Arrangements

Quite a number of manufacturers will offer drop-shipping arrangements. If you sell one of their items, they will ship it to your customer directly and you will pay them usually at a wholesale or discounted price. This works well in theory, but in practice you are placed at the mercy of the company doing the drop-shipping, since there may be delays in shipping the item, and in most cases you have little control over another company's shipping department.

You may also find many other people who have also entered into drop-shipping arrangements with the same company and you may be faced with a lot of competition; which will tend to make your profit margins very slim or non-existent.

One drop-ship arrangement which I would strongly advise you to avoid is one which levies warehousing fees to store the items to be drop-shipped.

So, my advice is not to jump into any arrangements until you have thoroughly investigated them and tested the market first before jumping in with both feet. Check them out on the Web. Dissatisfied customers can post some pretty nasty comments on the Web. I've seen some on automotive repair shops and auto dealers that would make your toes curl!

Hobbies

If you already have a hobby, such as stamp collecting or collecting antiques, you might want to consider developing this further into a business. There are many advantages to doing this, because you will already be familiar with the area and you will have less learning to do in order to get started. You will also be familiar with the current methods of selling and distribution.

Another advantage with developing a hobby into a business, if you are already working somewhere else, is that you can start the business slowly in your spare time until it has developed to such a stage that it can support you on a full-time basis.

Go online and search! You will probably find a ton of information that could help you.

Foreign Trade Commissioners

Whilst the embassies of most large foreign countries are located in Ottawa or Washington, consulates are often located in major cities around the country. Most of these have trade attachés who are responsible for developing trade opportunities with their home country. Such attachés can be a valuable source of information for companies in their homeland that are seeking representation abroad. E-mail them and find out if they can help you.

Buy on eBay Wholesale and Sell Individually

Several years ago, eBay introduced its wholesale categories and they have since enjoyed phenomenal growth. Basically, these allow manufacturers, wholesalers, distributors and retailers to sell large quantities of identical items. Most of these sell at significant discounts to their suggested retail prices and could be a fertile ground for acquiring products to sell on a one-at-a-time basis. Again, you really need to know the product area well and do your research properly.

Store Your Ideas

Even if you have selected an idea, it is still worthwhile creating a database which lists the ideas which you have collected. In the event that you have selected an idea which does not work out, you can always fall back on the others which you previously collected.

Negotiating Prices for Resale Items

You will have to be very hard-nosed when it comes to negotiating the price you are willing to pay for items for resale. For example, if you are offered a truck load of Super Widgets at a half price of $50 each, you may feel that you've got a bargain, only to find later that the same Super Widgets are selling on eBay for bids that close at around $40 each, which could generate you a nice loss of $10 each! So, my advice to you is to conduct lots and lots of research; get to know your market niche very well and be prepared to walk away from deals where you are unsuccessful in negotiating a price which could generate a profit for you.

Selling on a Consignment Basis

One way to reduce your risk, would be to locate manufacturers or distributors who will allow you to sell some of their items on a consignment basis. In other words, you don't purchase items from them until after you have sold them.

Make Sure Manufacturers Can Back You Up

Please make sure that the manufacturer or distributor can back you up. I remember, years ago I sold a number of very attractive wooden plant holders to major garden centres and when I ordered a whole bunch of them from the carpenter who made them, he told me he had discontinued. Boy, did I get egg all over my face but fortunately I had developed good relations with my customers and they were very forgiving.

On another occasion, a major security camera maker had provided me with a sample and pricing. I spent a lot of time, effort and money generating sales for the product, only to be told that they refused to sell to me because they had found that they were in conflict with a distribution agreement they had with another re-seller. That resulted in legal action but they sure settled out of court very fast in order not to tarnish their reputation.

Chapter 5

Use the Internet to Research Your Potential Market

Web Sources of Marketing Information

Aside from conducting a key word search (as I discussed in the last chapter), I performed a *Google* search on "Sources of marketing information" and turned up 1.84 million results, however, the initial listings did seem like very good sources of marketing information.

The Web Advantage

Some of the searches that I conducted above took between 5 seconds and 28 seconds to produce results. There was no cost. They were conducted from my office with no need to travel; to write letters or make phone calls or send faxes. I was able very quickly (in 30 minutes or less) to get a very good idea of what work had been done in this field. Indeed, the Web has transformed the sourcing of marketing information and it behoves you to use it to your advantage in conducting your market research.

The Importance of
Statistical Marketing Information

To many, statistics may remind you of some very boring classes at school, however, data from government census or other sources can be of vital importance in determining the size and potential market for your product or service.

US Census Bureau

The US Census Bureau offers statistical information which could be of interest. It covers several broad areas:

*   Economic Census
*   People and Households
*   Census Geography
*   Other Surveys and Data

The Bureau produces a Census on government every five years; an annual community survey as well as economic indicators which are released on an ongoing basis.

Public Information Office
US Bureau of the Census
4600 Silver Hill Rd.
Washington DC 20233-0001
Phone toll-free: 1-(800) 923-8282
Web site: www.census.gov

Statistics Canada (StatsCan)

Statistics Canada (StatsCan) is Canada's national statistical agency. It collects data and charts the economic, social and social cultural trends of the nation. Data is available to you in various formats, including an online service which features a daily news bulletin, called *The Daily*, with summaries of newly released data.

StatsCan can also provide you with detailed Canadian international trade statistics from a variety of sources. Its data collection includes major themes such as: agriculture, environment, health, manufacturing, prices, primary industries, social conditions, and travel and tourism. From these themes, they generate hundreds of publications and hundreds of thousands of data sets. For information on these, you should visit their Web site at: *www.statcan.gc.ca*.

Results from the 2011 Census of Population can provide you with information on age, gender, marital status, language, housing characteristics, ethnic origin, religion, education, citizenship, place of birth, labour force and income on a wide assortment of statistical products and services.

Topic-based tabulations can provide you with information which could be useful in determining your market size or for forecasting sales or for estimating the potential for your product or service. Statistical information is available on a wide range of topics.

Statistics Canada
150 Tunney's Pasture Driveway
Ottawa, ON K1A 0T6
Phone: (613) 951-8116
Fax: (613) 951-0581
Phone toll-free: 1-(800) 263-1136
TTY phone toll-free: 1-(800) 363-7629
Fax toll-free: 1-(877) 287-4369
E-mail: infostats@statcan.gc.ca/
Web site: http://www.statcan.gc.ca/

UK Office for National Statistics (ONS)

The latest Census was conducted on March 27, 2011.

UK National Statistics Online provides statistics for the United Kingdom.

These cover the following themes:

- Agriculture and Environment
- Business and Energy
- Children, Education and Skills
- Crime and Justice
- Economy
- Government
- Health and Social Care
- Labour Market
- People and Places

- Population
- Travel and Transport

Hub Liaison Team
Office for National Statistics
Room 1.101, Cardiff Road
Newport, South Wales
NP10 8XG
United Kingdom
Phone: +44 (0) 845 601 3034
Fax: +44 (0)1633 652747
Web site: www.statistics.gov.uk/hub

Eurostat Yearbook 2013

Eurostat Yearbook is published by the European Commission and is based on data provided by member states of the European Union. It is no longer released as a PDF file or as a printed book. Instead, it is available from its Web site and online databases which are being continuously updated as new data becomes available.

Eurostat Yearbook 2013 provides statistics relating to the countries which are currently members of the European Union together with some data for candidate countries.

Web site: http://epp.eurostat.ec.europa.eu

European Business: Facts and Figures

European Business: Facts and Figures features a series of articles which provide a comprehensive picture of the European business economy. They give a structural as well as enterprise class profiles together with regional analysis.

European Business: Facts and Figures is published by Eurostat:
Web site: http://epp.eurostat.ec.europa.eu

Get to Know Your Competition!

Before you can come up with a marketing strategy, it is essential that you study your competition. Find out who they are and how much of the market they control. Examine their marketing and advertising strategies.

The listings of marketing information mentioned previously can be invaluable in finding out about your competition.

Statistics Canada also publishes a series of "Small Business Profiles." These can be used to compare operating results of various types of small businesses from different locations in the country. They include figures about the companies such as average profits, expenses and sources of income etc.

In addition, information about any of your competitors that are publicly owned, can be obtained from their annual reports and from prospectuses and information releases that have to be filed with the various provincial Securities Commissions and you can access them on Sedar's web site.

The Corporations Branch of the federal Department of Consumer and Corporate Affairs in Hull, Québec also maintains files on public and private federal corporations. In the United States, Bloomberg can be very helpful in locating information about public companies.

Credit reporting companies, such as Dun and Bradstreet, maintain credit files on very large numbers of private companies. Some of these reports reveal interesting information on dollar volumes of sales and operating costs. Sometimes you may be able to obtain them through your bank (for a fee). Reports of this nature can help to reveal the total market size for an existing product.

Chapter 6

Choose a Great Name, then Register or Incorporate Your Business

Choose a Great Name!

Once you have decided on a product or service to offer, I would advise you to try and choose a great name for your business.

One way to do this is to find a name that relates to what you are offering. For example, I always remember the name "Two Men and a Truck" which is a franchise in the moving business. I also remember "Pizza Pizza" which even though it is blatantly obvious, is very catchy and great for running advertisements.

Another way is to combine the name with an Internet url. This has the advantage of helping to drive viewers to your Web site. For example, *"Learn2succeed.com Incorporated"* which is the pseudonym used by the author of this book and conveys the benefit of what this book and other books are about. It also allows for an expansion into video, audio and other learning products.

You could also use a cutesy name like "LuLuLemon" or "Alibaba" and even though many, such as these have already been taken, with a bit of imagination you could come up with your own.

Do yourself a favour: put the ego aside! Try not to use your name unless you can get it to convey a benefit e.g., "Mary's Gone Crackers" which is a great name being used for a line of organic crackers. Another example is the Ontario-based "George's Trains" which specializes in model railroads.

Take the time to come up with a good name. You are going to have to live by it!

Once you have selected a possible name or a number of them, you'll have to check to see that someone else is not already using them. First, search the Web. Second, have a name search company do a search for you. Many jurisdictions will require you to do this before you can incorporate. If you end up using someone else's name, you are leaving yourself open to being sued in court.

What Business Structure is the Most Suitable for You?

What type of legal structure is best for your situation? Be cautioned that there are also tax implications in your choice and you should seek professional advice.

The first type of business is a sole proprietorship. Here, you simply register the name of your business with the government for a relatively modest fee. You are then free to use the name which you have chosen and conduct business under that name.

The second type of business is a partnership which can involve two or more people. Under this type of arrangement the partners sign a partnership agreement which defines their ownership and responsibilities. Again, this type of business is relatively easy to form and, aside from the legal costs associated with the partnership agreement, registration fees are normally very modest.

The third type of business arrangement is to incorporate. This creates a separate legal entity which can have its own bank accounts and conduct business and enter into contracts as if it were an individual. The incorporated company is owned by the shareholders, who are issued shares reflecting their ownership. In addition, the incorporated company is expected to appoint a Board of Directors. The Board is responsible for determining the overall policies and directions of the company in addition to appointing the officers who run the company, such as the president, secretary, vice-president of finance, etc. The Board is also responsible for appointing outside advisers such as, accountants, attorneys or lawyers.

In a number of jurisdictions, it is possible for only one person to be the shareholder. In such a case that person would appoint themselves as the single member of the Board and occupy the positions of president and secretary.

In the United States it is also possible to establish what is known as a "C-Corporation", which allows the entrepreneur to start off in a proprietorship mode and then to switch to a corporate status once the company has advanced beyond the start-up stage.

Government Sales Tax and Vendor Permits

Once you have incorporated or registered your business you'll have to deal with the government's share. Don't forget that the government loves the sales tax revenues which your business creates. So, they will be out there looking for your contribution!

It is important that you get it correct right from the get-go. As you know, governments are almighty powerful when it comes to getting their share of the pie. In the US you will have to register for State taxes and obtain the necessary exemption permits. In Canada, you'll have to register for the Harmonized Sales Tax (HST) if you are in Ontario, New Brunswick, Nova Scotia, Newfoundland and Labrador. In the other provinces you'll need to register for provincial sales taxes and the federal Goods and Services Tax (GST).

If your business is unlikely to have sales of over $30,000, it is not necessary to register for the HST or GST, but if you are selling goods or services, you will have to register for a provincial sales tax permit (if you are not in a province that has HST) and collect taxes on your sales. When you are purchasing goods, you will be able to do so on a tax-exempt basis. In the US there is no federal sales tax (yet).

If you are selling jewellery, you'll need to consider excise taxes.

Don't forget about municipal taxes. The cities and towns want your money too!

Register Trademarks

A trade-mark is a word, a symbol, a design (or a combination) used to distinguish your wares or services from those of others in the market. It represents not only your goods and services, but also the reputation of your business. If you propose to use a Trademark, I would advise you to register it. In the US you can do this at the United States Patent and Trademark Office. In Canada, this can be done online at the Canadian Intellectual Property Office (CIPO). The Web sites are as follows:

USA: *www.uspto.gov*
Canada: *www.cipo.ic.gc.ca*

Chapter 7

Where to Locate Your Business

Home-based Businesses are a Popular Idea

IDC, a national research firm based in Framingham, MA, estimates that there are between 34.3 and 36.6 million home-based businesses in the USA Indeed the US Small Business Administration's Office of Advocacy estimate that more than 12% of all US households operate a home-based business. That means than on average, one in every eight homes you pass on a street operates a home-based business.

Recent numbers for Canada are hard to come by, but in 2003 there were 1.4 million home-based businesses according to Western Economic Diversification Canada, a Federal Government agency.

You will not be alone, if you are thinking of starting your own home-based business.

Home-Based Businesses are Survivors

According to the US Home-based Business Institute, if you operate a home-based business you are more likely than other business start-ups to survive the initial three-years. This is a critical time, because if you can't survive for the first three years; you're not likely to survive much longer. Indeed, the

Institute found that 70% of home-based business make it through this period, compared to only 20% for start-ups that were not home-based.

You certainly don't need a Ph.D. to figure out why the survival rate of home-based businesses is much higher than that for other start-ups. You've got to live somewhere, so if you can run your business off your kitchen table, you can save an awful lot of money on rent, your time to commute to work, baby sitting charges, and so on.

How Legal is it to Work Out of Your Home or Apartment?

Most residential leases prohibit the use of premises for business purposes, however, many landlords will turn a blind eye so long as the rent is paid on time and you don't disturb the neighbours. If it is a high traffic business, such as retail, where there are people constantly coming and going, there is likely to be trouble, especially when the neighbours start to complain.

Also, watch those municipal bylaws and zoning regulations! These are designed to restrict business to regulated areas and prohibit it in others. So if you're not in an area zoned for business, you are theoretically breaking the law. Again, if you don't flaunt it with lawn signs and lots of people coming and going, the chances are that nobody will notice.

Tax Advantages

Don't forget that there are some tax advantages if you use part of your residence as your principal place of business! You can use the rent relating to that business area as a legitimate business expense.

Be careful when you calculate the figures. The Canada Revenue Agency has become very finicky in recent years. They now want you to calculate how many hours you use certain portions of your premises for your home-based business. Obviously, if you have a room or certain rooms dedicated as offices, I feel that it would not be unreasonable to claim these on a 24-hour basis but I am not sure that the tax man will necessarily agree, so best to check with your tax accountant.

Also, the tax man wants to know what portion of your utility bills, municipal taxes, etc. are being claimed as business expenses.

If you use your car or truck for business (as well as pleasure) you can claim those expenses which relate to running your business. This includes insurance, repairs, lease payments. Again, your friends at the tax office have become very finicky, so my suggestion is to keep accurate figures of all your expenses and the number of miles or kilometres you log up on business and where you went. Keep these for when you complete your tax forms or for your accountant.

You can also write-off a portion of your entertainment expenses, provided that these are directly related to furthering the business. The portion that is allowed will vary from jurisdiction to jurisdiction.

Save on Commuting Time

I've run my own home-based business for over 29 years and one thing I love about it is the short commute time from the breakfast table to my office which takes about 30 seconds. Public transit can't get you to work that fast!

Indeed, Statistics Canada estimated that the average worker spends the equivalent of 12 full-days a year getting to work and returning home. The US Government claims that Americans spend over 100 hours per year commuting; which works out to about the same if you base it on an 8-hour work day.

Not only is an incredible amount of time wasted on commuting, there is the cost of transit fares which seem to keep going up at a relentless rate. If you know people who drive any significant distance to work in their SUV, I am sure you will hear them complain bitterly about the price of gas at the pump; not to mention the cost of parking.

Then of course are the hidden costs. Being stuck in traffic for hours getting to work is hardly conducive to making a great day! In fact, it probably increases your blood pressure, stress and other health conditions; not least of which is breathing in all the vehicle exhaust fumes.

All I can say is that I feel a lot of sympathy, when I look out of my window on a winter rush hour morning and look at row upon row of vehicles, bumper to bumper, slip sliding their way to work in the middle of a snow storm. Time for another coffee!

Commercial Space

You may need to give some thought to your location if you intend to lease commercial space. For example, if you are importing or exporting and are using air cargo for most of your shipments, then it might make sense for you to locate near the air cargo facilities of a major airport.

Again, if you are importing or exporting by truck or container, it could make sense to locate near to trucking terminals or container facilities. You will also need to consider truck level loading docks and make sure that there is enough room for a tractor trailer to back up to the door. I am amazed at the number of industrial units that offer truck level loading docks but have no room for the truck driver to back up!

Don't forget any other special features that you may have such as, dust free environment, special heating or cooling, any special water requirements or electrical--do you need 220 volt power?

Bricks-and-Mortar Retail Space

Location is one of the most important issues you will have to face in establishing your retail business.

If you have to rely on people passing your store to generate business, you'll need to locate in a high traffic area. Be warned, however, that landlords have figured out that they can extract a lot of rental money. So "Location, Location, Location" can also become "High Rent Costs, High Rent Costs, High Rent Costs!"

The question you will be faced with are high rent costs worth the traffic which may enter your store. More important, can you make a buck?

If you get it wrong, it can kill you. If you get it right, you can make a lot of money and... so will your landlord!

Watch Out for the Lease Renewal Trap

Unfortunately, I have seen the rent renewal trap all too often in business.

I remember a successful restaurant/deli called Oliver's located in the Yonge Eglinton area of Toronto. The owner served specialty breads and foods which could be consumed on premises in the restaurant but also taken out in the deli section. The place always seemed to be packed and I assume that business was good; especially since he was vertically integrated with his own organic farm which grew some of the produce.

Suddenly one day, the location was closed with a notice on the door thanking all his customers for their patronage but explaining that he was closing down because the landlord wanted so much of a rent increase that it wasn't worthwhile continuing in business.

I saw it with Bentley's original fish restaurant on Yonge Street in Toronto. It was also a restaurant/deli take out and it was forced to move to a smaller and less appealing location. The original premises remained closed for quite a number of years while the landlord looked for a new tenant.

I have seen it with a photocopy store on Eglinton Avenue in Toronto. A rent increase tipped the balance between profitability and loss. The business closed down!

So, when you are negotiating a lease, look well into the future. You don't want to spend five years busting your rear end to build up your business and then, when it comes to lease renewal time, your landlord wants to double your rent.

You are at the mercy of your landlord. Don't forget it!

Locating in a Mall

Most malls have one or more "anchor stores" or big retailers which draw a lot of traffic. That's the plus side.

The negative side is that you may have to surrender part of your profit to the mall owners. You will have to participate in advertising and other campaigns which will cost you money. You will have to obey all the mall rules, especially on hours of operation, signage, etc.

Also, watch out for the competition. The fact that you are a small fish in a big mall does not necessarily give you exclusivity. For example, if you are selling consumer electronics, a discounter in your same area may open up right opposite you and meanwhile you are tied up with a lease that you can't get out of.

Find Yourself a Good Lawyer

Before you enter into any lease, I would strongly advise you to consult a lawyer or attorney who is experienced with retail commercial leases. Please don't consult with your jack of all trades lawyer even if he or she costs a little less. It is imperative that you get proper legal advice. If the landlord won't agree to the changes you require, be prepared to walk away and start your search all over again!

Warehousing

An alterative to renting your own commercial space, is to use the services of a warehouse or storage company.

I have used a public warehouse service in the past and I have found the service to be very satisfactory, since I only paid for the space that I was using and this varied from time-to-time during the year. Also, they had the forklifts to move material to the loading dock where I could pick it up, as required.

I have also used public storage facilities, but in this case you rent a fixed caged space or pull-up "garage" space. The challenge is that normally you have to contract the space for a fixed period of time and you can't readily expand or contract. Also, if you live in the Northern US or Canada, you may find that working in sub-zero temperatures during the winter to be a bit of a drag. Of course, if you want to pay more, you can rent heated space.

Bonded Warehousing

A bonded warehouse allows you to store your imported goods without having to pay customs duties until they are released. Such facilities are available in the United States, Canada and most industrialized countries. Essentially, your goods are stored under bond. The terms may vary from jurisdiction to jurisdiction.

Chapter 8

Use the Internet to Source Your Equipment Needs

Equipment and Other Fixed Costs

Obviously, a major cost for many manufacturers is the equipment which they use and this may include vehicles. It may be possible to finance some of these or to obtain government assistance in the form of loans.

Vehicle and Equipment Leasing

Leasing is one method of financing your business, especially in the area of vehicles, computers and office equipment.

The size of the leasing market in the United States was estimated at $725 billion in 2013 according to The Equipment Leasing and Finance Foundation (ELFF). It estimates that the market will grow to $891 billion in 2015.

Leasing in Canada has gained tremendous popularity within the last few years and now accounts for 10% to 12% of all new equipment purchases; up from 4% just a few years ago.

According to the Equipment Leasors Association of Canada, leasing in Canada still lags far behind the United States where it accounts for 25% to 30% of all new equipment purchases.

Leasing can help you to conserve working capital. Your company does not have to lay out cash for the outright purchase of the asset and can use those funds for day-to-day expenses and operations.

Comparing leasing to equipment purchased on a financing plan; your payments are generally lower under the leasing arrangement. Also, most leases cover 100% of the equipment cost, including delivery, which is unlikely to be the case under a financing plan.

Leasing does not affect your firm's ability to borrow from your bank or other sources. The lease does not tie up any of your assets as collateral, simply because the asset does not legally belong to your business in the first place.

Your business can charge lease payments as operating expenses; thereby reducing taxes more than would have been possible by claiming capital cost allowances (under normal circumstances). Term of your lease can also be geared to the life expectancy of equipment in question.

Chapter 9

Use Your Computer to Prepare
Your Human Resource Plan

Human Resources

The topic of human resources is important and your business plan should include discussions on supervision and staff training. A break-down of your employee categories and the numbers in each should be provided.

Since salaries and wages form one of the largest expenses in any service organization, you should discuss these costs in detail, together with any incentive schemes.

Before preparing and determining your human resource requirements you may want to consider the advantages of subcontracting, computerization and factory automation.

Subcontracting

Subcontracting can prove to be an effective method of cutting your human resource costs in certain instances. This is particularly the case when the volume of work you have is insufficient to justify the full-time employment of a skilled person; or where expensive equipment is required in the preparation of an item.

You can use subcontracting with everything, from bookkeeping to metal cutting; from silk screening to injection moulding. In fact, subcontracting is very common in small business.

You may find that the unit costs of subcontracting are higher than performing the task internally; but the overall savings of not having to have a skilled person permanently on your payroll could be greater; assuming that the job is intermittent in nature.

In many instances, there may actually be savings in subcontracting. The subcontractor may have sophisticated equipment that will perform the task much faster.

An example might be a firm selling Masonite that will be cut to size for their customers. They may operate saws that will cut a large number of sheets at one time, which could make the job much cheaper than doing it in-house on a single sheet-by-sheet basis.

Because a subcontractor is being paid premium rates, productivity is often (but not always) higher. An added bonus may be that you get better quality of work and accuracy. The converse of the above argument is--do you have any idle equipment that could be used to subcontract to others? If so, could this generate added revenue for you?

Computerization

Computers were here long before Time Magazine ran a computer on its front cover as "Man of the Year." The difference is that they are now a lot less expensive and will do a great deal more. Computerization can lead to significant cost savings and could reduce your human resource requirements.

Factory Automation

Following initial successes in Japan; factory automation and robotics have gained an ever increasing toehold in North America. The cost of much of this technology is decreasing; whilst the software and sophistication is increasing. Many systems are now being designed for smaller business applications.

This technology can prove very cost-effective. Labour costs can be significantly reduced and quality greatly improved.

Determine How Many People You Will Need to Hire

Since wages are a major expense in most small businesses; especially those involved in providing services, you want to be careful not to hire more people than you need. You also don't want to hire too few, because if everyone is overworked, they will simply quit and go elsewhere.

If your needs vary according to the time of year, then I would suggest you consider hiring part-time help. For example, if you manufacture Christmas decorations, you may want to gear up production from mid-year until early December. If you operate a hunting camp, you'll need to hire people when the hunting season begins.

If your peak season is in the summer months, then student help could make sense since it will cost you less and you may be able to obtain some government assistance.

I would suggest that you calculate the number of full-time and part-time workers you will require, then prepare job descriptions.

Prepare the Job Descriptions

As its name suggests, a job description describes in detail the tasks, duties and responsibilities of a specific employee. It should also state the contribution you expect that employee to make and define the outcome that you expect.

Once you have done that, you will need to determine what skills or qualifications are needed for the person occupying the position. Don't get carried away on the qualifications–if you need a scientist, sometimes a person with a Ph.D. can be very academic and not necessarily suited to working in a competitive, cutthroat business environment. Business experience often counts more than a string of degrees.

Salaries and Hidden Costs

Once you have prepared the job descriptions, you need to figure out how much you are willing to pay by way of salary. When determining this figure, don't forget the "hidden" costs such as vacation pay, sick leave, workers compensation payments for workers who are injured on the job. In the US, you may be required to contribute towards health insurance; depending on your location. In Canada, you are also expected to contribute to an employee's health insurance plan and, as an employer, you are also required to contribute to the worker's Canada Pension Plan (CPP) and Employment Insurance (EI).

Third Party Liability

If you are providing a service, where your employees are working outside of your premises, you will need to seriously consider carrying third party liability insurance. The easiest way to illustrate this is to consider an installer of surveillance cameras. Say he is installing a system in a jewellery store and his ladder falls over and smashes a showcase full of expensive ceramic figurines. Obviously, your employee and your business will be held liable and you could be sued. If you carry third party liability, your insurance should cover the cost of the damage.

Honesty Bonds or Fidelity Bonds

Another aspect of your human resource plan should cover bonded employees. This is especially necessary if you have employees who work off-premises. What happens if they steal something belonging to your customer? A fidelity bond will guarantee the honesty of your employee.

Intellectual Property and Non-competition Agreements

Let's say that your employee has created a new gizmo. Does this invention belong to you or to the employee? If it is done while he or she is working for you, then it should belong to you but it is best to get it in writing.

Also, if your employee suddenly quits, you don't want them opening shop across the street selling the same gizmo. In this case, getting your employees to sign a non-compete clause would be reasonable but don't forget that you cannot prevent him or her from earning a living. So, best to talk to your lawyer first.

Pay Equity

As you are aware, there is much gender-based discrimination in the workplace and as an employer, you want to be sure that you offer equal pay for work of equal value. If you want to learn more, I would refer you to the book *Salary Administration* which can be purchased securely online at *www.ProductivePublications.com* in the United States or at *www.ProductivePublications.ca* in Canada.

Employment Contracts

In some instances, you may want to enter into an employment contract with a new employee. This basically sets out the terms and conditions of the relationship between your business and your employee. It is commonly used by employers to fill positions left vacant by women away on maternity leave.

It could also be used in cases where you are employing the services of a freelance worker, such as a graphic designer to prepare brochures, advertising material or Web pages.

Are Employee Share Ownership Plans a Dream?

Could this be a dream? Employees who arrive early for work; stay late without demanding overtime; never take sick leave; have perfect quality control and display unnerving loyalty to corporate well-being!

Or, could this be the demented fantasy for you, after a frustrating day of management by crisis? Maybe it is the latest offering of a steel collar worker from the catalogue of Toshiba's System Robots?

It might be none of these! It could be the product of an ingenious twist of capitalism that places share ownership in the hands of workers. Employee Share Ownership Plans or "ESOPs" as they are commonly referred to, provide a mechanism whereby employees can participate in the fortunes of the companies for which they work.

The evidence for increased worker productivity is supported by the release in 2008 of a research study by Brent Kramer, a doctoral candidate at the City University of New York, which "provides strong evidence that majority employee-owned businesses have a significant advantage over comparable traditionally-owned businesses in sales per employee." Indeed, if averaged out, employees in majority-owned ESOP businesses produced $44,500 or 8.8% more per employee in annual sales than employees in companies without such a plan. It's not a dream–it's reality!

How Can ESOPs Help?

There are two aspects to employee participation in the ownership in your business.

The first, is the sense of pride which employees obtain from knowing that they own part of your business. This helps ensure maximum profitability for your firm.

The second aspect is the true financing of your business. This is especially true for early stage companies, if you do not have the cash to pay for high calibre or skilled employees, but are able to make up part of their wages in the form of stock. This was the case with Apple Computer, when it first started, and resulted in a number of their employees eventually becoming millionaires.

There is also a story about a cleaning lady at Canadian Tire's head office, in Toronto, who joined such a plan at an early stage and was rumoured to be a millionairess when she retired. The funny thing is that she never told her husband about it!

Types of ESOPs

You should distinguish between two different types of ESOPs.

One type comes in the form of options to purchase shares at a fixed price at some future date. A Toronto Stock Exchange study found that 54% of the companies listed on the Exchange offered participation to their employees in the form of such "option plans."

The other type is a "share plan" which allows your employees to voluntarily purchase shares. Financial assistance is frequently offered by your company to facilitate the purchase and in some cases the shares may even be bought outright on behalf of the employee.

Share plans are less common. Thus, the Toronto Stock Exchange study found that only 23% of their listed companies had such plans.

Share plans come in two varieties. Either the employee owns the shares directly or the shares are put into a trust and held in his or her account.

It has been suggested by two authorities on the subject (Donald Nitingale of Queen's University and Richard Long of the University of Saskatchewan), that direct ownership is more effective than holding shares in a trust.

Performance Bonuses

You could offer your employees a performance bonus. This could be based on the performance of your business as a whole or a department. This works well when your business is prospering but can lead to a lot of discontent if your business does poorly or there is an economic downturn.

Your Human Resource Plan

If you bring together all of the elements that I have just discussed, you have the basis for writing your human resource plan. Essentially, it should cover:

- your goals and objectives;
- the number of people you require;
- the skills level of those people;
- their experience;
- any legal considerations such as non-competition clauses;
- legal liabilities and honesty bonds that are necessary;
- budget that you have available to pay them including the "hidden costs;" and,
- any incentives that you may offer such as bonuses or ESOPs.

Chapter 10

Use Your Computer to Prepare Your Advertising and Marketing Plan

The "Blur" Between Marketing and Advertising

In the minds of many people, "marketing" and "advertising" are synonymous. This is not strictly correct because marketing involves the whole method of distribution, pricing and getting the product into the hands of consumers. Having said this, advertising is an important component of marketing.

Let's examine what they encompass in more detail.

What Marketing Encompasses

The American Marketing Association has defined marketing as "the process of planning and executing the conception, pricing, promotion and distribution of ideas, goods and services to create exchanges that satisfy individual and organizational objectives."

In the case of a physical product, marketing involves more than just "advertising"--it involves getting that product from the place where it is manufactured into the hands of the consumer, plus all the planning and pricing considerations.

In the case of a digital product, you could deliver the goods electronically over the Internet. This could be the case for software, electronic newspapers, magazines, e-books, music, videos, photographs, etc. In addition, there are planning and pricing considerations that have to be taken into account as part of the marketing process.

What I said above is also applicable to services. Whether it be those offered by a stockbroker, a banker, an accountant, a professional house painter, a dentist, an insurance agent, etc. They all have to let the consumer know of their existence and what they offer, which is the advertising component. They also have to let the consumer know about the price of their service and obviously, how it is delivered.

What Advertising Encompasses

According to Wikipedia, advertising is a form of communication that typically attempts to persuade potential customers to purchase or to consume more of a particular brand of a product or to use a service. It can assume many forms, as you will see in the following chapters, but in almost every instance the advertiser is paying for the message.

The type of communication can take many forms, all the way from material posted on the Web, to newspapers, magazines, radio, television, as well as signs and billboards. In the following pages, I'll take you on a tour of different methods of delivering your advertising message. This tour is oriented towards those of you who are either thinking of starting a business or are already operating a small business.

The Advertising Market is Not Homogeneous

One of the most important distinctions to make is between advertising to business, on the one hand, and advertising to the consumer, on the other.

"B2B" stands for Business-to-Business transactions. It is a term that has become popular in the Internet era and **usually** refers to e-commerce transactions but can **also** refer to transactions where e-commerce is not involved.

"B2C" is an acronym for Business-to-Consumer transactions and once again, can refer to both online and offline transactions; although it usually refers to the former.

Crafting the Message

The creative process is of the utmost importance in crafting a message that can be delivered by the medium you choose to employ (print, television, radio, Internet, etc.). You may want to engage the services of commercial artists, professional photographers, recording professionals, video cameramen and editors with experience in creating advertising content. Alternatively, you may wish to engage the services of an advertising agency which can pull all of the elements together for you. This need not be as expensive as it sounds, especially in our soft economy and the professionalism of some of these talented people can be well worthwhile.

Whether you are doing it yourself, or employing outside talent, there are several steps you must take.

First of all, you have to know to whom you will be delivering the message. Are you targeting teens, retired people, women, men, professionals, financially sophisticated, or other groups? In other words, you need to develop a profile of your intended audience.

Secondly, you will have to choose the most appropriate medium to reach that target audience. Thus, if you are selling inks for commercial printing machines, you may want to advertise in some of the magazines that are targeted to printers and the graphics trade. If you are selling a book on trading stock options, you might want to advertise in the financial press or on cable television such as the Business News Network (BNN). Alternatively, you may want to advertise in different media at the same time. Thus, if your budget permits, you could advertise in both newspapers and cable television.

You have to create an effective message which relates to that target audience. What are the "hooks?" Are you appealing to emotions and if so, which ones? Which major benefits do you want to emphasize? What tone do you want to employ: do you want to be aggressive, laid back, sensual, and so on?

Delivering Your Message

Where is your audience located? Obviously, you are not going to advertise an agricultural tractor to city folk, nor are you likely to advertise a shoebox sized automobile, that will fit into the tiniest parking spot to country folk.

You also have to decide on when is the best time of the year to deliver your message. Take some obvious examples. If you are located in a northern climate, you would want to advertise barbecues in the spring, skiis in the winter, gifts before Christmas.

If you are using television or radio, you also need to consider the best time of day to deliver your message. Spaghetti sauce before dinner, antacids after dinner!

Try to Create a Sense of Urgency

In my own opinion, if you can create a sense of urgency, your advertisement will be much more effective than one that contains no sense of urgency. Thus, you could be advertising a "limited time offer," "only while quantities last," "your last chance" and so on. If possible, try to get people in your target audience to do something...to act now.

Having said this, it is not always possible to include a message to motivate people to act. You may only want your advertisement to show that your products are superior to those of your competitors so that your product will be favoured the next time your potential customer visits a retail store. This goes back to your objectives: what are you trying to achieve?

In the end, you want to influence people so that they have a favourable impression of your product and its benefits. If you can create a sense of urgency, so much the better.

Your Marketing Strategy

The objective of developing a strategy is to position your company in such a way as to gain a competitive advantage in the marketplace. According to Andrew Campbell of Campbell & Associates, "this includes having the right product in the right market at the right time with the right price..."

Methods of Distribution

As part of your marketing strategy, you will have to decide on the distribution method that is most appropriate for your product.

Many people have invented great ideas but they never made it because there wasn't a distribution system that could get them into the hands of the people who needed them at realistic prices.

The market demand also has to be large enough to support your product. Take an absurd example: mink coats for poodles. It is almost certain that there are some rich widows out there who would invest in a mink coat for their favourite canine. The question is: would a pet store owner carry such an item for one in a million chance of a sale to his poodle-owning clientele?

There are many ways to distribute product or to market services. These include direct sales using your own exclusive sales force to sell direct to the customer or to the retailer.

You could also use a sales representative who also reps other lines or you could use a distributor.

You could sell by direct mail or by means of advertisements with clip-out coupons in newspapers, magazines or periodicals. You could use radio or television to solicit orders.

Trade shows and fairs offer opportunities for you to sell direct to the end consumer.

Telemarketing has gained considerable popularity in recent years, however, some computerized automated messages have roused considerable public ire and you may want to avoid using such methods.

You should consider these and other methods of distribution. The questions you have to ask yourself are: Will they work? What is the best one? Could more than one approach be used? Here is where test marketing could be very helpful to you.

Pricing

Your test marketing can also be used to test different prices in different markets. It does not always follow that the lowest price is the one that achieves the highest sales volume for you.

Sometimes, consumers will pay a higher price in the belief that the value is greater. A classic in this regard was when the cold medicine *Contact C* was first test marketed, volume of sales of the product bearing a price of $1.69 was three times higher than that of the same product bearing a price of $0.99.The reason was that when people are sick they want the best, and a higher price implies "the best."

This example should caution you to be careful in avoiding the trap of cutting prices in order to increase volume. Don't make the mistake of attempting to increase sales by discounting. Remember, that a big profit margin on a low sales volume can often be better for you than a slim profit margin on a high sales volume!

Marketing "quality" often means selling at higher prices than the competition.

Pricing is a function of demand for a product relative to its available supply. The introduction of the Cabbage Patch Doll a few years ago provided a classic illustration of high price associated with scarce supply which lasted during that introductory period.

Pricing is also a function of "elasticity" of the product--how necessary is it? Basic foodstuffs and shelter are relatively "inelastic" insofar as people have to have them. Luxuries such as computer games or Cabbage Patch Dolls are very elastic because people can exist quite well without them.

Packaging and Merchandising

Packaging is vitally important; especially for many lower ticket items. It is the package that often helps sells your product.

Laundry detergents may have very similar or identical characteristics so far as the consumer is concerned, however, it is often the packaging that assists the consumer in making a final choice. Mind you, this is frequently done in conjunction with price.

If you are developing a product where the packaging is important, try to make up some dummy cartons or packages. Get some art students to do some rough layouts for you and paste them onto the boxes.

If you have the time and the money, try different types of packaging and vary the colours and then do some tests to see which one people like the most. Document the results and use them in your marketing plan.

If your product lends itself to being sold in a merchandiser or display of some type, then consider making a sketch of your merchandising stand and construct a sample if possible.

Image

A professional image counts a great deal, especially in the service and retail industries. You should consider uniforms, caps, logos, painted vans and anything that will help to enhance your status as a provider of that service.

If you ever have to seek outside financing, from a bank or an investor, they are more likely to be impressed if you have given some thought to this matter.

What could be worse than having to admit that your staff drive up to a customer's residence in a rusty old van and are dressed in tattered jeans?

Advertise on the Internet

The Internet allows smaller companies access to a much wider geographical area than they might currently serve. Any company or any person anywhere in the world that has Internet access could become a target for an advertising campaign and at the moment that means about 1.5 billion people...and growing at over 300% a year–a phenomenal rate.

There is the question of language. Not everyone speaks English and as Internet usage expands around the world, it will become an electronic Tower of Babel and marketing people will need to address this challenge in the future.

Notwithstanding this limitation, the Internet could greatly increase the geographic advertising reach of most home-based, small and medium-sized businesses.

Your Advertising and Marketing Plan

Put all the information that has been discussed into one document and you have your advertising and marketing plan.

This document should include results of your market surveys, your competition, the strengths and weaknesses of your product versus theirs. Include your marketing strategy and how you intend to distribute your product. Mention pricing and packaging and any test marketing which you may have done. Give consideration to your proposed advertising methods and to lead generation and promotion.

Chapter 11

Create Your Own Web Site and Sell Online

The World is Your Oyster

William Shakespeare may not have thought about it this way when he uttered this phrase back in 1600, but the World Wide Web (www) or "Web" brings the world to your doorstep and enables you to view documents from around the world. As you know, it will deliver text, images, photos, sound, animation and videos.

From a business viewpoint, being able to advertise and sell your products or services over the Web makes it a very valuable marketing tool. So, in the first part of this chapter, I'll show you how to establish your own presence on the Internet by setting up your own Web site and then I will devote the rest of it to the topic of e-commerce to show you how to sell your own products online.

Register Your Domain Name

There are over a quarter billion domain names registered worldwide. It's a crowded field and most of the good, "snappy" single-word names have already been taken.

If you've already registered or incorporated your business, it would be advisable to use that name as a domain name, so long as it is still available. To find that out, simply go to any of the Web sites of companies that will register domain names for you (against payment of an annual fee) or the WHOIS site at *www.whois.net* and enter the name you want to register. If it's not available, I would suggest selecting something that reflects the product or service which you offer.

Create Your Own Web Site

There are many "consultants" who can design a Web site for you. Some of them do an excellent job–some of them do a lousy job. Some of them don't charge much–others are outrageous. My own observation is that most of them are very heavy on the graphic arts; the fancy stuff but are not very strong when it comes to creating an effective e-commerce site i.e., where visitors to your site can buy your products or services and pay for them.

If you decide to do-it-yourself, you'll need Web authoring software to create your Web site. (I'll discuss this later in this chapter.) Once you have created your site, you "upload it" over your Internet connection to the server of your Web hosting company.

Web Hosting

When you create a page or a document with your word processing program, you'll probably save it on a hard drive and you can view it again at any time in the future by opening the file. Similarly on the Internet. Your Web pages are stored on the server at your Web hosting company site and visitors can access them using your Web address (URL) on their browser. In essence, your Web pages are "files" which can be retrieved from the hard drive on the remote computer that is hosting your site.

Adobe Dreamweaver

All in all, *Dreamweaver* is a very powerful Web authoring tool. It has gained a large following, especially amongst Web developers. The product will also appeal to you if you prefer to work in a visual editing environment.

Microsoft FrontPage

Unfortunately, *Microsoft FrontPage* has been discontinued but I must admit that I still use it and I really like it. Fortunately, old versions can still be purchased over the Internet.

The program was designed with the users of *Microsoft Office Suite* in mind, since it provided many of the familiar tools from that suite. This gives you a familiar environment to work in.

Publishing your Web site is fairly straightforward. Obviously, you need a Web hosting company to host the site for you. If you need to make revisions to your site, you have the option to only publish those pages which have changed or to re-publish the whole thing.

Web Easy Professional

Web Easy Professional 10 is published by MySoftware (Avanquest) and provides you with an easy way to create your own professional looking Web site using drag and drop. It features over 1,000 template combinations and allows you to add *GoogleMaps* and link buttons for *Facebook* and *Twitter*. You can even add audio files if you have a microphone and a recorder.

Web Studio

Web Studio is an introductory package that lets you quickly create your own business Web site and post it to the Internet. It requires very little experience to use since it gives you assistance in creating your own layout by using a number of templates that are supplied. You can modify them and customize the layout to fit your particular needs and drag and drop your graphics or animations to the places where you require them.

If you are a beginner, this introductory product will help you create your own Web site very quickly, however, it does not feature the high level of sophistication of some of the other programs which I reviewed in this chapter.

Your Shopping Cart

A "shopping cart," exactly as its name implies, is an electronic cart in which the shopper places the goods which he or she wants to purchase. In order to add products to this cart, the shopper would click on an "add to shopping cart button" and state the quantity required of a particular item. Most e-commerce programs will permit shoppers to view the contents of their shopping cart at any time by clicking another button: "view shopping cart."

Your Checkout

The second basic element in e-commerce programs is the "checkout" where, just as in a supermarket, shoppers have the opportunity to verify what they have selected and pay for their purchase, usually using a credit card.

Your Methods of Receiving Payment

The most generally accepted method of payment for electronic commerce transactions made over the Internet is by means of credit cards. The three main players in this market are VISA, MasterCard and American Express.

As you are probably aware, you will have to establish your business as a merchant that can accept payment using one of these cards. This usually involves a credit check and other verification to establish your authenticity as a viable business. In some instances, the credit card company may require the posting of a security deposit which can be from $5,000 or more; depending on the transaction volume of the business. The good news is that the deposits will earn interest, however, the bad news is that this is usually very minimal.

If you are a merchant with a relatively low volume of transactions you can often clear these over a touch-tone phone; using an Interactive Voice

Response (IVR) system. If you have higher volumes, you may have to rent a terminal.

Another way of approaching credit card transactions is to employ the services of a third party to perform the credit card authorizations and transactions for you.

Payment Gateways

Probably the best definition of a payment gateway comes from PayPal: "a payment gateway provides a secure connection between your online store and your Internet merchant account."

There are many payment gateway providers but the following provides brief reviews of some of the major players in this area.

PayPal Payment Gateway: is one of the largest. Even though it is now owned by eBay, it will still process payments securely for online merchants who do not use eBay. One point of interest is that PayPal has introduced a new fee structure to accommodate micropayments of under $2.00. I understand that this is 5% of the value of the transaction plus a fee of 5¢ per transaction. Further information can be obtained at *www.paypal.com*.

WorldPay: is another major player which lets you accept payments by phone, fax or mail. It can facilitate credit and debit cards, bank transfers, instalments and even mobile payments. It can facilitate payments in most currencies and in many languages. For further information, go to *www.worldpay.com*.

Authorize.Net: boasts of a customer base of 350,000 merchants and its services are sold through a network of reseller partners and financial institutions. Further information can be obtained at *www.authorize.net*.

InternetSecure Inc: is a Canadian company whose gateway has been approved by all six major Canadian banks. It offers a secure Canadian and US dollar, online credit card processing system for internet merchants. It is conducted in real-time and accepts VISA, MasterCard, American Express and Discover cards. Further details can be obtained at: *www.internetsecure.com*.

Offer Alternative Ways
for Your Customers to Order and Pay

Since many customers are still averse to giving out their credit card numbers over the Internet, I would suggest that you also offer them alternative ways of making payments. This can be as simple as asking them to send a cheque in the mail or send a fax which includes credit card information i.e., card number, expiry date and name of card holder. In order to facilitate such orders, it would be helpful to give your customer an order form to fill out. In this way, all the credit card and other essential pieces of information can be collected, including shipping address, any special instructions and a phone number in case writing cannot be deciphered, or in case of delivery problems. Such an order form can be offered in the form of a PDF file which can be downloaded from your Web site.

Another way to facilitate payment is to allow your customer to call on a toll-free line or other phone number so that the credit card information can be given over the phone. Obviously, this requires the presence of someone at your place of business to accept such orders, since leaving credit card information on a voice mail system is not a good idea because the security of such systems can often be breached by hackers. In fact, I would strongly advise you to post a message warning your customers not to leave credit card information on your voice-mail system since you could get embroiled in disputes with both your customer and the credit card company in the event that this information is stolen by some outside party.

In the case of companies that have widespread presence in many cities, such as Wal-Mart, Sears and the major automobile manufacturers, customers could go to the nearest physical outlet to complete the financial transaction and pick up their goods. Obviously, this is an option that is not available to most small businesses that may only have one business location.

In summary, you want to try to offer your customers as many ways to make payment as possible so that they can choose the one that is most convenient for **them**; rather than the one that is most convenient to **you**, the merchant. Remember, that the "Customer is King" and the more enjoyable your customer's shopping experience is with you; the more likely they are to return and buy more.

International Transactions

Don't forget that when you open your e-commerce Web site, you are inviting people from all over the world to do business with you. This brings with it a number of challenges. The first deals with the currency of the transaction, the second with sales taxes and customs clearance and the third, deals with fulfilment i.e., getting your product into the hands of the consumer. These are all factors you must consider when establishing an e-commerce site.

Security of Transaction

The security of transactions is a major concern to consumers using the Internet. In most cases, these fears are unfounded, especially with the encryption technology that is being used by most Internet merchants. In spite of this, the perception still persists in the public mind that the Internet is not a secure place to conduct financial transactions and this is exacerbated by headline news when fraud does occur (even though most bank robberies, which occur at a fairly high rate of frequency in major cities, go unreported).

Fulfilment

Once you have the order, you have to get the goods into the hands of the customer. Obviously, if the "goods" are in digital form such as digitized photographs, digital music or videos, an eBook, etc., they can be downloaded directly by the consumer once payment has been verified.

In most other cases, you will have to pack and ship the goods and this usually presents very little problem for domestic shipments within Canada or the USA, but can be more challenging for items you have to ship overseas. Indeed, for low cost, bulky or heavy goods, you may find it uneconomic to consider exporting them because of high freight costs.

Main Types of E-Commerce Software

Insofar as my discussion in this book is concerned, there are three main types of e-commerce software that you can use as a small business and that are not exorbitantly expensive.

The first lets you use plug-ins which can be used in conjunction with one of the Web authoring packages such as *FrontPage* or *Dreamweaver*. I discussed each of these authoring packages earlier in this chapter. Essentially, you lay out your pages using one of these Web authoring programs and then you add the shopping cart. This will provide you with "add to shopping cart" buttons together with a check-out system which I described earlier.

The second involves the use of stand-alone e-commerce software in which you create all your Web pages in the program itself, together with all the necessary buttons and forms required for commerce. Essentially, these stand-alone products are "Web authoring" tools specifically geared to e-commerce. An example is *ecBuilder* which I will cover later in this chapter.

The third group involves the use of a hosted e-commerce solution provided by a specific service provider such as Kagi, Hostway or even your own eBay store (which I will cover in this chapter). Microsoft made an attempt at this with its *B-Central*, however, abandoned it in August 2004.

Many of the other remaining e-commerce solutions are much more elaborate and also more expensive; especially those which require you to install your own servers.

In the following text I'll give you a quick look, first at the plug-ins, then at stand-alone e-commerce software and finally some of the solutions which involve a specific service provider.

Just Add Commerce (JAC)

Just Add Commerce (*JAC*) by Rich Media Technologies of Savannah, Georgia, offers brilliantly designed and simple to use plug-ins for both *FrontPage* and *Dreamweaver*. The software can be downloaded directly from the company's Web site. It is also relatively inexpensive; considering its capabilities.

This JAC system also allows you to host your Web site with any ISP or hosting company because JAC does not have any server-side requirements.

I was very impressed with JAC and would highly recommend this plug-in to anyone who has authored their Web pages in *FrontPage* or *Dreamweaver* because it allows you to create and structure your Web sites according to your specific needs and requirements, and then add the appropriate "Add to Shopping Cart" or "View Shopping Cart" buttons. It is also very simple to use–I've been using it for several years now--definitely a winner!

WebPlus

WebPlus by Serif is a Web authoring software package which has e-commerce features included.

121

This program is published by Serif and is a relatively inexpensive solution if you want to create a professional looking Web site. The program comes with tutorials which are very simple to follow and can help get you up and running very quickly.

StoreFront.net

StoreFront was originally produced by LaGarde, Inc. before its acquisition by Dydacorp which is located in Parsippany, New Jersey.

StoreFront offers you a number of Web design templates together with access to a team of professional store design professionals. It permits you to have an unlimited number of products. You can also create discounts.

It is a sophisticated program but the last time I checked, it had a fairly steep sticker price of about $500 per month, plus credit card processing fees and Web hosting fees.

SalesCart Express

The original *SalesCart* by ComCity Corporation was a feature-rich e-commerce add-on to *FrontPage 2000* or *FrontPage 2002*. It has since been replaced by *SalesCart Express* and works as a plug-in with *Microsoft Expression Web* or *Adobe Dreamweaver*. In other words, you design your own Web site using *Microsoft Expression Web* or *Adobe Dreamweaver* and then you add *Salescart Express* to perform the e-commerce functions.

To accept payments, the program features *PayPal Express* check out which is included. Alternatively, you can use *AuthorizeNet* or *USAePay* gateways; however extra fees apply. The last time I checked, the cost was relatively modest at $25 per month with a $50 set-up fee.

ecBuilder Pro

ecBuilder Pro is a software package which enables you to build the front-end of your online store. It provides you with 40 templates to choose from, according to your type of business. You can then list an unlimited number of items.

The whole process is conducted by filling out about 14 screens of information. Next comes the time-consuming part of entering all of your products, descriptions and prices. *Version 6* of the software provides gateways to seven payment processors.

SiteLink

SiteLink is an e-commerce solution which is tightly integrated with *MailOrder Manager* (*M.O.M.*) It features a number of templates to help you design an online store or you can design your own. The strength of this program is that it draws on all the taxation, product information, inventory levels, etc., already contained in your *M.O.M.* database.

Actinic Catalogue

Actinic Catalogue is published by Actinic Software and boasts of being the UK's leading shopping cart software with 6,800 active online store users. It offers you pre-made templates and permits you to enter up to 10,000 products. As with *ecBuilder*, it provides a payment gateway but only to three providers.

Storecreator by Volusion

Storecreator is available as a download from *www.volusion.com*. You have a choice of different versions which can handle anywhere from a store with 100 products to one with an unlimited number.

If you have up to 100 products for sale, *Storecreator* can be a relatively inexpensive program.at $15 per month.

PDG Shopping Cart

PDG Software, Inc. from Tucker, Georgia, offers you a number of e-commerce solutions ranging with an increasing range of capabilities, as follows.

PDG Commerce Lite: which sells for under $600 US and can handle up to 100 products. For slightly under $200 you can obtain the services of a consultant to assist in linking your storefront to *QuickBooks*.

PDG Commerce Pro: which sells for under $1,000 US and can handle up to 1,000 products. For slightly under $200 you can obtain the services of a consultant to assist in linking your storefront to *QuickBooks*.

PDG Commerce Gold: which sells for under $1,400 US and can handle up to 5,000 products. You can also obtain the services of a consultant at no cost to assist in linking your storefront to *QuickBooks*.

PDG Commerce Platinum: which sells for under $1,800 US and can handle an unlimited number of products. Again, you can obtain the services of a consultant at no cost to assist in linking your storefront to *QuickBooks*.

PDG works with many of the major credit card authorization companies and offers security of transaction.

Kagi

Kagi of California offers a hosted e-commerce solution. In other words, you set up your store on the Kagi site and place your shopping cart buttons on your own site; linked to the products in your store.

Kagi has been in business for over 19 years and specializes in selling electronic products online. It is not geared to sell physical products.

From your customers' viewpoint, they accept all major credit cards as well as payments by PayPal. Probably the easiest way to get a handle on this is to visit the Web site associated with another business which I own:

www.eBooks2succeed.com. Click on one of the "BUY" buttons and you will be directed to our products in the store.

One great advantage of using Kagi is that you can establish affiliates and supply them with affiliate IDs. Kagi will remit their portion of payments directly to them.

I've used Kagi for some time now and have found them to be very helpful during the set-up.

Hover

Hover also offers several flavours of its hosted Web solution. The first is a "Starter" which is a Web site of 10 pages or less. The next two; namely "Basic" and "Website Extender" offer you unlimited pages, however, the latter enables you to build *Facebook* pages and a responsive mobile Web site.

The system makes it easy for you to create a Web site in minutes from a number of templates and without any previous experience. The monthly costs are very reasonable.

To conduct e-commerce, Hover offers an add-on for all of its FlexCloud Site hosting plans for slightly less than $10 USD per month.

I have attended one of their presentation seminars and I have to say that I was impressed with their product, however, you will have to be prepared to work within the design parameters which they establish. On the other hand, the pricing seems to me to be very reasonable and certainly challenges a lot of the other e-commerce solution providers.

Become an Amazon Merchant!

Amazon has become famous for its print and eBook offerings but it has also strayed into other areas and it is now possible, as an Amazon Merchant, to basically open up a "sub-store" as a "merchant" and sell your products under their umbrella. In fact, Amazon has even gone so far as to sell grocery items from its *AmazonFresh* site at a few select locations. With grocery margins so small, I have to question whether this was is smart move, unless you want to load your grocery cart with CDs to make it worth their while!

For full disclosure, my business is an Amazon Merchant for softcover books in both Canada and ths US, but do not assume that a listing on Amazon will result in truckloads of money being dumped on your doorstep! It's a tough slog and Amazon extracts its pound of flesh by way of fees. Also, Amazon makes you do all the work in creating your listings!

You have a choice of paying on a per-transaction basis or paying a monthly fee. In return, Amazon processes the credit card transactions and remits payment to you after awhile.

You are responsible for shipping the goods. If you don't ship in a timely manner, you will end up with a poor rating which customers can see in advance before they purchase. So, it pays to ship promptly!

You will be able to obtain a lot of information online about becoming an Amazon merchant, however, there are a number of cautions that I would like to add.

Firstly, Amazon works in separate "silos" from a geographic viewpoint. In other words, *Amazon.ca* and *Amazon.com* are separate legal entities. Being listed on *Amazon.ca* does not automatically mean that your products are listed on *Amazon.com*. You can indicate on your *Amazon.ca* listings that you are **willing** to sell to the US but how many Americans are going to search *Amazon.ca* for what they want? So, here's the catch. If you are Canada-based, you will have to set up another account with *Amazon.com* at an additional monthly charge of $39.99. Also, since you are set up on *Amazon.ca* under one legal name, you may not be able to use the same name in the US and in my case, I have to operate in the US under the name of an affiliated business.

Under your agreement with Amazon, you can either ship the goods yourself or have them shipped by Amazon under their Fulfilment by Amazon (FBA) arrangement.

Be cautioned, that if you have Amazon do the shipping, you will have to absorb the cost of shipping to one of their warehouses plus you will have to absorb their warehousing fees. On the other hand, your end customers will be able to take advantage of freight discounts which Amazon offers as well as the free freight which is offered on shipping for orders over a certain value.

If you decide to do your own shipping, Amazon will give you a shipping allowance. This may be adequate for expedited or express items, but it can be woefully inadequate for items sent by regular parcel post. If you are a Canadian business selling into the US you will find that the $3.99 shipping allowance will leave you well short changed since most items you ship by Canada Post to a US destination are likely to cost $14 or more. If you have enough profit margin to absorb the $10 difference, you will be alright but, if not, you could be in trouble on every sale. For your information, I have complained bitterly about this and was told verbally that Amazon was no longer accepting complaints about the matter! "Let them eat cake" seems to be their attitude!

If you are a Canadian business with listings on *Amazon.ca* you will receive payments by direct deposit on a timely basis less bank charges! If you are selling through *Amazon.com* you will find that Amazon refuses to send any money due to you by cheque and insists on direct electronic deposit by Automated Clearing House Settlements (ACH) transfer. Now that may sound fine and dandy, but only a few Canadian financial institutions offer this service and the monthly service fees are in the range of $45 to $50 per month PLUS the service fees to maintain the bank account, PLUS your Amazon fees! This can be relatively inconsequential if you are making gross profits of $500 or more per month but if you are making less than that, it can take a significant chunk out of your profits. Again, Amazon refuses to issue cheques to Canadian merchants. "Let them eat cake!"

On the plus side, you will be able to get great exposure for your products.

Other Shopping Cart Software Programs

If you are serious about developing an e-commerce capability for your business, you may want to take a look at several other alternatives as follows:

- *ShopSite Pro*
- *MerchandiZer Pro*
- *MonsterCommerce Pro*
- *Mercantec Softcart*

- *GoEmerchant I-store*
- *Miva Merchant*
- *X-Cart Pro*

Chapter 12

Cash Flow is Your Lifeblood!

Why are Spreadsheets so Important?

I am going to age myself! When I first started in business, spreadsheets were just starting to make their appearance–mostly in larger companies and especially in the financial industry. Now they are everywhere. Indeed, I would find it almost impossible to run my businesses today, if I did not have access to spreadsheet software. For example, I use spreadsheets for banking, accounting, for sales taxes, for production, for calculating authors' royalties, for orders, for keeping track of inventory; to name but a few.

Spreadsheets help me do my job much more efficiently and in a fraction of the time it would take using a desktop calculator. A number of years ago, when I ran the spreadsheet special interest group at my local computer club, I found that many of the small business members were keenly aware of how spreadsheets could help them but sadly, when I look at some of my business friends and suppliers, I find that many of them have not taken the trouble to master the software.

My advice is that if you want to plan your business and be successful, one of the first steps to take is to learn how to use a spreadsheet. There are many courses available. Instruction manuals have improved tremendously. Even the companies that publish the software have made it much easier to learn how to use their products.

What are Spreadsheets?

Probably the simplest explanation of a spreadsheet is that it is a document which enables you to organize data into rows and tables. It then enables you to manipulate and massage the data. To give you some idea of what spreadsheets can be used for, the following list of ready-made templates were featured in an earlier version of *Quattro Pro*.

Reporting

- telemarketing reports
- receipt for goods reports
- commission reports
- daily production reports
- expense reports
- marketing personnel expenses
- parts inventory
- petty cash reports

- product lines sales
- production reject report
- project cost summary
- property and estate
- receiving reports
- sales activity reports
- store for store sales
- summary of key accounts

Forms:

- telephone sales orders
- daily time sheets
- deposits to a sum
- invoice record

- monthly auto expense report
- service invoice
- shipping order
- vendor master file

Financial:

- income statements
- inventory
- perpetual inventory control
- quarterly cash flow
- weekly cash flow

- sales promotion expenses
- statement of cash flows
- statement
- 7-year balloon loan

Analysis:

- vendor cost analysis
- sales trend analysis
- real rate return on investment
- breakeven analysis
- debt ratios
- liquidity analysis

- present value
- profitability ratios
- sales channel analysis
- sales adjusted seasonally
- sales trend analysis
- vendor cost analysis

Preparing Projections:

- moving average sales forecast
- new product sales forecast

- the payback period
- pro-forma balance sheet

Budgeting and Planning:

- estimating start-up capital
- year ended tax planning
- expense budget

- merchandise plan
- product sales goals
- quarterly marketing budget

- trade show budget
- the year end tax plan

Corel Quattro Pro

I've been using *Quattro Pro* for many years now. One of the tremendous strengths of the *Quattro Pro* package is its ability to create charts and graphs very readily from the data in your spreadsheet. This is important because it is sometimes hard to get an overall view of what is going on from rows and columns of numbers in a spreadsheet. When this information is presented graphically, I find it much easier to understand what the figures mean. All in all, *Quattro Pro* is an excellent spreadsheet program.

Microsoft Excel

Another titan in the spreadsheet area is *Microsoft Excel*. This is also a very sophisticated package which will allow you to do a great many things.

Lotus 1-2-3

Lotus 1-2-3 is another very powerful spreadsheet program. It was the first to gain widespread market dominance when the personal-computer first made its appearance. Indeed, it became (and still is in many instances) a standard used by many large businesses and government organizations. Unfortunately, it seemed that Lotus management fell asleep at the wheel and were so busy basking in their success, that they failed to recognize that other products (such as *Quattro Pro* and *Excel)* were catching up with and eventually overtaking them since they offered better solutions from a technical viewpoint.

Lotus was acquired by IBM a number of years ago and now flies under the IBM banner. In common with *Quattro Pro* and *Excel*, it can be used to transmit data to Web sites. It also has strong charting features.

OpenOffice Calc

In 1999, Sun Microsystems acquired *StarOffice*, a software suite which commanded about one-third of the German office suite market. As a part of its marketing strategy, Sun Microsystems originally made the suite available to users at no cost, however, but after Oracle's purchase of Sun, the software was re-named *"Oracle OpenOffice Calc"* and became part of the *Oracle OpenOffice Suite*. In June 2011, Oracle donated the code of *OpenOffice* to the Apache Software Foundation's incubator. It provides you with all the basics that you need for doing fairly straightforward spreadsheet work.

Use Cash Flow Projections to Calculate Your Needs

Much has been written about cash flow but probably the best way for you to envisage it is to go to a bathtub analogy.

Imagine the tap is fully open and water (cash from sales or the money which you put into the business) is rushing into the tub. Then, imagine that the outflow plug is only partly open. The water that is flowing out represents the money that you are spending on capital equipment, overhead, wages,

135

inventory etc. It has gone. The water that is left in the tub (if any) represents the money that remains in your bank or in cash and can be used to expand your business.

Let's take the analogy a step further. Assume that you want to float your favourite rubber duck (in this case your company) in the tub. If there is sufficient water, the duck will float and likewise will your company, if there is sufficient cash. However, if the water is flowing out of the tub at a faster rate than it is coming in, the duck "ain't going to float" and so it will be with your company--the receiver will come in and kick you out of the bathroom!

Change the design of the tub a bit! Let us say that there are two taps providing water. The "capital tap" provides your start-up capital. In the case of a lender, it is called your "loan tap." It may also be a combination of them. Let's call the other tap the "sales revenue tap." This delivers the revenue from the sales of your products or service and includes the profit which you have made.

Before you start, there has to be some water in the tub for the duck to float. If you haven't made any sales, that water will have to come from the capital or loan tap. Once you start selling your product or service, the water from the sales tap may keep the duck afloat without any more water from the other tap. If not, one of three things will have to happen.

Either the flow of water out of the tub (expenses and production costs) will have to be reduced or the flow of water from the sales tap will have to be increased by increasing your prices or by selling more. Alternatively, more water will have to be supplied through your capital or loan tap.

The water that has to be added through that capital or loan tap to keep the duck afloat represents the minimum amount of money that has to be put into your business to make it work. This simple analogy represents a simplification of the concept of cash flow, but illustrates how vital it is to the survival of your business. Let's examine this for an initial two month period:

MONTH ONE	
CASH BALANCE AT BEGINNING	$0
ADD CASH COMING IN:	
Cash from entrepreneur	$25,000
Cash from sales	$0
Total cash coming in:	$25,000
TOTAL CASH AVAILABLE	$25,000
LESS CASH GOING OUT:	
Machinery purchase	$10,000
Rent	$1,000
Office supplies	$100
Telephone & answering	$100
Inventory	$5,000
Wages	$4,000
Selling & advertising	$1,800
TOTAL CASH GOING OUT	$22,000
CASH BALANCE AT END	$3,000

MONTH TWO	
CASH BALANCE AT BEGINNING	$3,000
ADD CASH COMING IN:	
Cash from entrepreneur	$0
Cash from sales	$3,000
Total cash coming in:	$3,000
TOTAL CASH AVAILABLE	$6,000
LESS CASH GOING OUT:	
Machinery purchase	$0
Rent	$1,000
Office supplies	$100
Telephone & answering	$100
Inventory	$1,000
Wages	$4,000
Selling & advertising	$1,800
TOTAL CASH GOING OUT	$8,000
CASH DEFICIENCY AT END	($2,000)

Let's examine this in a little more detail.

If this is your company, it is actually making $1,200 ($3,000 minus $1,800) on its sales, however, when overhead (rent, office supplies, telephone) are subtracted, together with the costs of purchasing more inventory and wages your will actually end up with a cash deficiency of $5,000. However, there was $3,000 brought forward from the first month, so the cash deficiency is reduced to $2,000.

Where is the money going to come from to cover your deficiency? Are wages going to be cut back, is more product going to be sold, will the price of your product have to be increased or will you have to put more money into the business?

What happens if you do not have any more money? Maybe you can borrow it or maybe you can find an investor. By that stage it may be too late–your employees have already quit when they didn't receive their pay cheques!

The time for you to find all this out is in advance. Create cash flow models, such as this and keep repeating until you find out if the project will fly on its own with your own money or if you will have to go outside to look for cash. The exercise will also allow you to obtain an idea of how much you realistically require to put your show on the road.

I must emphasize that the above discussion is very much simplified. Things like trade credit can affect the figures quite dramatically.

Taking the above example again, if you offer trade terms of 30 days on sales of your product and assuming that, in practice the money is not received until 60 days later, this means that your cash would not be received until the third month. Your company would then have a cash deficiency of $5,000.00 in the second month.

This is a very important fact that many start-up entrepreneurs ignore at their peril. I have certainly found this to be the case when I have been acting as a consultant to early-stage firms.

Will Your Cash Flow be Adequate?

The question that you have to ask is whether there is enough water flowing into your bath tub from your profit tap to keep your proverbial duck afloat entirely, without having to add more water (or money) to the tub.

Maybe it is best to qualify what I mean. Most businesses require some initial capital, for example, a window washing service company will probably need squeegees, detergent, pails, a ladder and if he is high minded, a rope, a pulley, a mobile scaffold (and lots of courage).

The question you have to ask is if, after that initial expenditure, can the business run itself without additional capital being added?

"After the initial expenditure?" you say. "And if I spend a million dollars initially? The trouble is--I don't have the dough!" Herein, lies the trap in my generalization. By self-financing, I am making the assumption that the initial seed capital is relatively modest.

Let me go back to the window washing example. Assume that for the first job, the window washer borrows a bucket and a ladder. He goes to Canadian Tire and purchases some detergent and a squeegee. He's in business!

When he collects enough money he buys his own ladder and bucket. The assumption I have made in this chapter is that the initial requirements are relatively modest and can be financed internally; out of pocket, without the necessity of approaching outside sources.

If you are launching a high-tech business, it is likely that your initial capital requirements will be much greater and this may mean that you will be forced to seek outside financing.

Chapter 13

Use Your Computer to Find Out How Much Money You Will Need to Start

Can Your Business Finance Itself?

About 9% of start-ups finance themselves from internally generated cash. A study by Venture Magazine showed that this form of financing provides more than twice the amount of capital obtained from venture capital sources (4%) and almost twice that from private placements (5%).

An Ontario Government study found that only about half of all new business owners required additional capital after they had started. The implicit assumption is, that the other half were generating sufficient funds internally to sustain themselves and to expand.

Figures from Statistics Canada indicate that, for companies with annual revenues of under $5 million, 36.5% of their capital requirements come from internally generated funds.

Indeed, if you can make enough high-tech mousetraps in your basement (using your own seed money to build them) and load them in the back of your car, you may be able to sell them directly to the end users at a handsome profit.

You could use the money you made from such sales to employ somebody to work in your basement for you while you go out on the road selling. This will allow you to produce more, since one person is now fully occupied in manufacturing. The additional money which you make may allow you to hire a second person for production...then a sales representative.

Your next step might be to find a small manufacturing space that is inexpensive. This will allow you to employ three more people in production and put a second sales rep on the road. So on it goes!

Some Preliminary Considerations

Before you can determine whether the business will finance itself, you have to look at your own available resources. Does your company have the resources in the form of manpower and equipment etc., to go it alone and achieve your strategic objectives? If it has, then by all means sail your own ship because this is the cheapest form of capital you can possibly obtain.

What is Bootstrap Financing?

Bootstrap financing is the method of generating capital from the internal operations of your company. In essence, the financing is provided by your business without the involvement of any outsiders. There are no bank loans; no participation by venture capitalists and probably the only initial injection of cash was from your savings, as the owner. Thereafter, your show runs itself without your having to rely on financial partners. You can wake up in the morning and not have to worry about whether your bank is going to call your loan. It provides you with freedom from outside interference that may have attracted you to do "your own thing" in the first place.

You can finance by bootstrapping to develop your company to a stage when it becomes attractive for outside financing.

If you bootstrap finance your business, you may not be able to grow it as fast as it might have with the assistance of outside financial help. It can only grow as fast as it can generate enough money for expansion. So, bootstrap financing could be a severe limiting factor on the speed of your growth.

Bootstrap financing requires a substantial amount of control over your business operations. For example, you have to be vigilant to ensure that the monies owing from customers (called "receivables") are coming in promptly to finance your growth.

If you don't have controls in place, then things can become so fouled-up that the financial health of your company may be jeopardized and any potential growth stunted. Bootstrap financing requires that you manage your business in the fast lane to be really successful.

Can You Supply Your Own Capital?

In the case of start-up and early stage financing, personal resources are very important. An Ontario Government study found that two-thirds to three-quarters of the average start-up investment of $25,000 was put up by the entrepreneur himself or herself. These figures clearly demonstrate a lack of readily available outside financing for companies at the start-up stage.

In the case of established small and medium-sized growth companies, a more recent study by Statistics Canada reveals that 29.9% of financing for such companies came from internally generated funds or retained earnings.

The Personal Financial Statement

The easiest way of coming to a decision as to whether you have enough money or not, is to prepare a personal financial statement in order to determine your true financial position.

To achieve this, you will need to calculate your personal assets (what you own) and your personal liabilities (what you owe).

ASSETS	
Cash in bank or savings	
Stocks or bonds at market value	
Real estate at market value	
Automobile at market value	
Other assets at market value	
TOTAL ASSETS	

LIABILITIES	
Bank loans	
Mortgage	
Credit card balances	
Installment purchases	
Personal taxes due or owning	
Any other financial commitments	
TOTAL LIABILITIES	

In arriving at your net worth, you will want to subtract what you owe (your liabilities) from what you own (your assets).

You can now compare this final figure with the financial requirements of your business. At this point, it becomes a personal judgement call as to whether or not you will go ahead using your own funds or if so, what portion of them you will commit to your business.

If you have sufficient assets, you may be able to obtain a personal bank loan, but watch out if your bank wants you to pledge those assets as security for the loan.

A Question of Comparative Risk

Banks generally insist on excessive collateral (security put up by the borrower in return for a loan or debt), especially for start-up situations.

A University of Western Ontario study found that personal collateral requirements from the owners approached four times the amount of money that was being loaned. Yes, FOUR times!

For companies with annual sales of under $250,000 the personal requirement was about two and a half times. Companies with higher sales volumes required less personal commitment, however, it was only for companies with annual sales of over $2 million that the requirement fell marginally under 100%.

All this sounds fine if your new business makes a lot of money and the bank gets paid back. The trouble starts if this doesn't happen and your bank wants to pick up on the collateral which has been pledged under the personal guarantees.

If you take a fictitious situation where you own a home valued at $400,000 and you have pledged it for a $100,000 loan. The bank could come in and seize the home, whereas, one might have been able to raise the $100,000 through a mortgage (even a second or third) on the house. Whilst the loss of the $100,000 that was obtained from the mortgage might be quite painful for you, it might be a lot less painful than having the bank seize your home and anything else that was posted under your guarantee.

Banks also tend to become nervous when the value of the collateral pledged starts to drop in value. Thus, if your $400,000 home decreased in value to $250,000, reflecting some dip in the economy, you may find your bank manger tightening the reins quite a bit.

In certain cases, going to the government for money may help you avoid the personal guarantee, however, many government loans also insist on the posting of personal collateral.

Outside Financing

Venture capitalists and angel investors may be reluctant to invest in your start-up or early stage company and, if they do, they are likely to want a large portion of the ownership. The same venture capitalists, however, may be quite willing to invest in your business at a later stage when it has shown that it is profitable. At this point the amount of ownership that you have to give up is likely to be much smaller.

Financing While Working Elsewhere

Many a wise person has started a business on the side, whilst working for somebody else. Such an arrangement can provide you with a temporary cash flow (over and above living expenses) to float your new business.

The big disadvantage, if you do this, is the lack of time which it allows you to start your business properly. As you will likely find out, a new operation

149

requires hours and hours of dedicated work and total commitment. You may find this very difficult to make, if you also have to spend eight hours working for someone else to bring in the bacon.

Credit Cards

It may sound facetious, but people have actually financed their start-ups with cash advances made on their credit cards!

The advantage to you is that no collateral is required and no approval is necessary for what you use the funds. The disadvantage is that interest rates are usually very high and you have to pay the money back, even though this may be in stages--just as with any other money you borrow. Enough said!

Love Money

"Love money" is the term used to describe investments made by relatives and friends.

It is a significant source of financing for start-ups. According to an Ontario Government study, relatives and friends provided 15% of the start-up funding for the incorporated companies studied and 31% for the unincorporated ones.

A similar study in Venture Magazine suggested that loans from relatives and friends accounted for 11% of the capital for start-ups.

Canada's classic example of an entrepreneur who raised financing from "love money" was the inventor of the game *Trivial Pursuit*. It is reported that Derrick Ramsey, then a copy boy for the Montreal Gazette, invested $1,000 in this scheme only to find his investment grow to $1/2 million!

You could look to your friends and relatives could be looked to for direct small cash investments or for loan guarantees. However, if your venture goes off track and ends up in the swamp, you may wake up one morning to find that, not only do you not have a business, but you don't have any friends or relatives left either!

I'll offer some anonymous advice from Evan Esar's *20,000 Quips and Quotes*: "Neither a borrower or a lender be: if you're a borrower, you'll have distant relatives; if you're a lender, you'll have close ones."

And I'll provide you with some advice on where to find wealthy relatives: "Some relatives are distant, some are close, but the wealthiest are both distant and close." You are on your own on this one!

Equity Crowdfunding

In essence, crowdfunding is a process in which pools of small financial contributions are made via the Internet in order to raise capital for an initiative, project or enterprise.

The US Securities and Exchange Commission (SEC) and the Ontario Securities Commission (OSC) have both fallen into a regulatory quagmire of trying to protect investors on one hand while allowing small businesses and start-ups to get easy access to capital.

In Britain, the Province of Saskatchewan, Australia and New Zealand have adopted more enlightened regulations with respect to equity crowdfunding.

If you want to learn more about it, I would encourage you to read: *Crowdfunding for Beginners: How to Raise Money for Start-Ups, Early Stage Enterprises, Charities and Non-Profits* which can be purchased securely online from *www.ProductivePublications.ca* in Canada or *www.ProductivePublications.com* in the US or overseas.

Chapter 14

Use Your Computer to Prepare Your Business Plan

Prepare Your Plan!

If you have been diligently following the ideas presented in this book, you should now be in a position to bring it all together in the form of your business plan. There's another book published by the publisher: ***Business Planning for Beginners: Find Out How Much Money You Will Need to Run Your Business***. It can be purchased securely online in the United States at ***www.ProductivePublications.com*** or at ***www.ProductivePublications.ca*** in Canada.

There are also a number of business software programs for business analysis and planning purposes. The good news is that competition has helped to drive down prices.

Plan Write

Plan Write is published by Business Resource Software of Austin, Texas. It can be used for Internet, manufacturing or service businesses.

One very strong feature is that you can customize your plan and this helps you to create a plan which looks unique as opposed to a plan created by using a "cookie cutter." This is important if you are making presentations to potential investors or lenders. I would highly recommend it for beginners to create a plan that is customizable and unique to your business.

PlanMagic Business

PlanMagic Business is published by the PlanMagic Corporation which was one of the first companies to enter the business planning software area back in 1994. Initially, they created a business plan template. Since then the company has developed a full product line of business planning and analysis software which encompasses marketing planning with marketing goals and strategies, operations planning, advertising and promotion, product mix analysis, pricing strategy, risk management and several others. I wish I had been able to lay my hands on *PlanMagic* before I had attempted to write my first business plan many years ago!

PlanMagic Non Profit

PlanMagic Non Profit is not too dissimilar to *PlanMagic Business* with the obvious difference that it is oriented towards non-profit organizations.

Business Plan Pro Standard Edition

Business Plan Pro by PaloAlto Software is a very powerful, completely self-contained package that helps you create a plan in simple steps. An

"EasyPlan Wizard*"* asks you a number of questions so that you can select a plan outline or adapt one of the 500 sample plans contained in the package.

Canadian Edition: of *Business Plan Pro* covers GST and HST issues as well as offering industry information which is specific to Canada.

UK Edition: of *Business Plan Pro* is specifically designed for businesses in the UK and also includes a database of UK and EU venture capitalists.

The company claims that *Business Plan Pro* has been the best-selling business planning software over the past 10 years.

Business Plan Pro Premier Edition

Business Plan Pro Premier Edition is a more sophisticated (and expensive) version of the basic package; featured above. It is designed so that you start a new plan based on your previous year's data. In this way you can continuously revise your plan over a multi-year period as circumstances change. You can also compare the projections you made with what actually happened in reality.

Jian Biz Plan Builder

You might also want to take a look at *Jian Biz Plan Builder*. This provides a cunning way of coming up with a professional looking business plan without having to learn any additional software other than Microsoft *Word* and *Excel* which you may currently be using.

To help prepare you for the time when you are being grilled by potential investors or lenders, it helps you to address in advance many of the common questions such people will ask. Most importantly, this software helps you write your plan from the viewpoint of the potential lender or investor.

Use Your Plan if You Are Seeking Outside Funding

Use the Executive Summary or overview of your plan to approach potential investors. If they are interested, then be prepared to send the full plan.

You will probably find, in making presentations with a business plan, that the investor who says that you have a nice plan probably is not a serious contender. The one who picks the plan to pieces, challenges your ideas, your integrity, your sanity and everything else is more likely to be your investor.

The first presentations will soon give you a feel for your plan and whether any revisions are required. Listen carefully to the questions asked and the criticisms offered.

Allow for Modifications

Maybe your plan needs clarification in certain parts or maybe it needs additional information. This is why it is best fo you to prepare short photocopy runs rather than blowing the company's cash reserves in the local print shop on a massive one-time printing.

In listening to criticisms of your plan, do so with discretion. Some people just love the challenge to tear things apart, for the sake of tearing them apart, whereas others will offer constructive criticism. It is this latter group that you want to listen to and when the same point comes up at different meetings, you know that some revision may be necessary.

Your business plan will be your basic document for seeking funding. It may be necessary to make modifications to cater to certain groups. For instance, in seeking provincial government funding, officials will want to know what the benefits are to the province in question e.g., the creation of more jobs. The Federal Government may be interested in export markets or the replacement of imports, effects on the environment, etc.

Successful Group Presentations

If you are going to expose yourself to the venture capital community, you are likely to be called upon to present your plan to a group meeting. The time slot you may be allocated can run anywhere from one minute through to about twenty minutes at the most.

If you are an accomplished public speaker, you will be able to sail through these events with flying colours. Most entrepreneurs, however, have limited experience in this area.

A survey published in *Current Opinion* found that Americans were more afraid of public speaking than of death, illness or poverty!

It is very important that you try hard to overcome any shortcomings you have, so that you create a favourable impression during the few minutes that you are allotted to present your idea.

The key word to all successful presentations is "preparation."

It's hard to distill the details for an entire company's operation, product lines and strategies into a talk lasting only a few minutes. Start with the Executive Summary or overview from your business plan and trim it down to the main points.

Some chairpersons are quite strict in enforcing the time allocations and there is nothing worse than to find that you are halfway through your presentation when you are cut off.

Practice your presentation using a watch and a tape recorder and make sure that you are not talking too fast. Even better, try practicing in front of a video camcorder and review your performance afterwards. If you don't have one, practice in front of your wife or the family dog--but get it down pat!

Have your presentation typed in large letters and double-spaced. Try to use single sheets that are not stapled together, so you can flip them over easily as you turn from one page to the next.

Have the script there with you on the podium in case you need it, but try to practice making the presentation without referring to it--this will give you an air of confidence and help to impart to your audience that you are an expert on the topic under discussion.

If you are addressing a large group, it is not necessary to make eye contact with everyone--rather keep your eyes focused slightly above their heads as you look around the room. This way everybody in the audience will feel included.

Take your time! When your turn comes, don't rush to the podium as if you are competing in the Olympics. When you get there--pause before you start talking. This helps to gain the attention of everyone in the room.

Don't talk too fast or too slowly (normal conversation speed will do it) and make sure you are speaking into the microphone!

And finally, dress well and conservatively, try to look reasonably happy, relaxed and confident! If you still can't manage it - take a course in public speaking or refer to the book *Public Speaking for Beginners: How to Communicate Effectively in the Digital Age* prepared by Learn2succeed.com Incorporated and published by Productive Publications. It can be purchased securely online in the United States at *www.ProductivePublications.com* or at *www.ProductivePublications.ca* in Canada.

Chapter 15

Track Your Progress
and Be Prepared to Modify Your Business Plan

Monitoring and Altering Your Strategic Objectives

Unfortunately (or fortunately, depending on your viewpoint) things don't stand still. As I alluded at the beginning of this book, we are afflicted by the ancient Chinese curse: "may you live in interesting times!"

Change presents you with difficulties (or "challenges") in the strategic planning process. The economy is changing; prices are changing; customer needs are changing. If everything is changing--how can you plan?

The smart answer is that your planning should take into account the possibility of change. But, what if the change is unexpected? Again the smart answer--strategic planning should take into account the possibilities of something unexpected happening. For instance, if a key employee, who has been healthy all his life, suddenly has a heart attack. Can somebody take his place?

Sudden change is difficult to monitor. It either happens or it doesn't! Gradual change, on the other hand, can and should be monitored. Such changes are likely to have an effect on your strategic objectives. If your objectives are rigid and hewn in stone, then they may prove to be unattainable. To put it another way, it is no use for you to keep shooting in the same direction after somebody has moved the target!

Responding to change is a little like shooting at a moving target. You have to alter the gun sights to account for different distances and you also have to change the direction the gun is pointing in.

Change may make your objective closer or (as is normally the case) further, in the time horizon. You may have to change the direction of thrust as the corporate goal changes. If the target or objective disappears altogether, then it is time for you to sit down and think the whole thing through again!

All that has been said thus far is of no use unless changes are monitored and plans are altered or modified in response to them.

Change is not bad. If it was not for change, many opportunities would not present themselves to you. Taking advantage of change can present you with enormous potential possibilities for growth.

Take the typewriter as an example. The manual version was replaced by the electric. The electric was then replaced by the electronic. In turn, the electronic has now been replaced by the word processor and personal computer manufacturers and manufacturers of computer printers have just been waiting for everybody to get there!

In trying to attain one of your strategic objectives, it does not matter how many times you have to alter your plan--the main thing is to get there. Tenzing and Hillary knew their objective was to climb Mount Everest. They had planned their route but they still had to make little detours as they approached their objective.

As a small business or start-up owner, you must be prepared to modify your strategic objectives in the light of emerging realities. In so doing, you may discover other windows of opportunity for your products or services.